Qanon and The Dark Agenda

The Illuminati Protocols Explained And The Arrival Of A New World

Simon Smith

1

Disclaimer

All erudition supplied in this book is specified for educational and academic purposes only. The author is not in any way responsible for any outcomes that emerge from utilizing this book. Constructive efforts have been made to render information that is both precise and effective. Still, the author is not to be held answerable for the accuracy or use/misuse of this information.

Foreword

I will like to thank you for taking the very first step of trusting me and deciding to purchase/read this life-transforming book. Thanks for investing your time and resources on this product.

I can assure you of precise outcomes if you will diligently follow the specific blueprint I lay bare in the information handbook you are currently checking out. It has transformed lives, and I firmly believe it will equally change your own life too.

All the information I provided in this Do It Yourself piece is easy to absorb and practice.

Table of Contents

INTRODUCTION

The Illuminati is either a "conspiracy theory" or a "conspiracy fact," depending on who you talk to. Those acquainted with the Illuminati society may tell you that it is a wicked and criminal network of some of the world's most educated, wealthy,elite leaders, business people, and political leaders, who work behind the scenes to gain and maintain high levels of power, enormous wealth, and wield control over the world. The list of claims that occurred with this monstrous conspiracy is extensive, and also range from the Illuminati being an elite good-old-boy network watching out for their interests (often in unethical ways) to claims that they are alien beings from another galaxy who masquerade as people, drink the blood of people to make it through, and are working to prepare the earth for the arrival of the Antichrist who will rule and control the New World Order as a god, using those who praise him "immortality" through transhumanist technology merging machine with a man.

This book is written to assist you in getting to the core of the conspiracy by providing you with some of the initial evidence proving the existence and activities of this infamous group, going back to the late 1700s in the state of Bavaria, Germany, and as a growing number of evidence is stacked up, we will slowly move into the recent times, showing beyond reasonable doubt that the Illuminati is still completely functional, and a lot of the "conspiracy theories" are in fact, very true.

This analysis will investigate and analyze the numerous accusations and conspiracy theories related to the Illuminati. Because the subject is so large, this second volume was required to continue my analysis of the extensive claims and evidence linked to the "Illuminati conspiracy." I am dedicated to separating the realities from the fiction, showing that facts within the hill of "conspiracy theories" are well distributed on this subject, there is a considerable quantity of irrefutable evidence that there is undoubtedly a powerful "Illuminati" secret society that is running today in America and worldwide.

There is also a large amount of wild speculation, lies, and half-truths about what the Illuminati is doing, who is involved with them, and what evidence is offered. Some individuals dismiss the idea that there is a "conspiracy" and do not even think such a thing exists, because when an informed. Rational person stumbles upon a few of the more outrageous allegations originating from the Illuminati conspiracy; they shake their head in disbelief and conclude that all the claims and "conspiracy theories" have to be incorrect as well; thinking such requests must have come from mentally psychopathic people who claim a few of the more far-fetched and made-up information as "proof" and "evidence.".

In this book, I will offer you a rational approach to the concept of an "Illuminati conspiracy," I will discuss the historical evidence of the genuine Bavarian Illuminati and the roots of this secret society spawned countless tales of its power and reach.

I will likewise cover many affiliated secret societies and will continue to investigate different individuals who claim to be real previous members. The book will also take a look at some elite political insiders and see what they have to say about the Illuminati and the belief that a secret society of men is posing a risk to the world and our flexibilities.

Doubters of an Illuminati conspiracy will be very shocked to see the names of some popular individuals throughout history who have made stunning statements plainly showing their conviction that the Illuminati is genuine and creates a threat to all of us.

I do not like to use the word "conspiracy" because it has a negative connotation that it is simply a "conspiracy theory. The terms "conspiracy theory" and "conspiracy theorist" have ended up being pejorative, which indicates they have a negative connotation and are used to insult people and shut down the discussion, comparable to someone shrieking "racist" at someone in efforts to bypass important thinking and cause a knee jerk reaction to paint them as such, when in reality they merely have an opposing ideology on a specific issue.

Much to some people's surprise, lots of "conspiracies" are true, and the dictionary meaning of a conspiracy is "an agreement by two or more individuals to perpetrate a criminal offense, scams, or other wrongful act." Individuals are charged with "conspiracy" in criminal courts every day for merely "conspiring" or planning to engage in a criminal activity.

Conspiracies do happen on a small scale, such as when two individuals conspire to steal or rob a bank, and on a large scale when a country's leader creates a reason to go to war.

Conspiracies are a fact of life. When researchers point out real and irrefutable evidence that exposes a conspiracy, they are often attacked or labeled as "hat-wearing conspiracy theorists," because the term causes people to dismiss the claims as a paranoid deception imagined by someone on the Internet who resides in their mother's apartment. The reality is that genuine conspiracy theorists can be found in high positions of power, and well-read individuals put forth conspiracy theories. Let's not forget that Hillary Clinton openly declared that a "right-wing conspiracy" was fabricating claims that President Bill Clinton had a sexual affair with intern Monica Lewinski. Hillary Clinton was just being a conspiracy theorist, when in reality, her other half Bill was having sexual relations with the intern, and there was no conspiracy attempting to bring him down-- it was only individuals reporting on the truth.

The Bush administration came up with a conspiracy theory that Iraq had weapons of mass destruction and were getting set to use them on America and allies, thereby attacking the country based upon this conspiracy theory, which was later shown to be

100% false. Not just was it incorrect; it was a lie cooked up to justify the invasion and war. As everybody now understands, there were no weapons of mass destruction at all, and Americans had been fooled into fighting based upon a conspiracy theory made up by the United States government.

Until the twenty-first century, a lot of Americans had never heard of the Illuminati. Dan Brown's novel Angels & Demons somehow introduced people to the group in 2003 (although his version was more like a purposeful disinformation campaign). And with the advancement of the information age, social media such as YouTube videos and many websites becoming committed to the subject, more individuals have started to learn about it.

The 2004 election in America brought John Kerry and George W. Bush together to compete for the presidency, both of whom are members of the Skull & Bones secret society headquartered at Yale University, which somehow added fuel to this growing fire.

This was how two Skull & Bones members were able to secure the nominations for both the Democrat and Republican parties in the same election, so no matter which one of them won (George W. Bush or John Kerry), it would be a success for Skull & Bones.

It was around this same time that "9/11 conspiracy theories" were growing, and the cover story for the War in Iraq continued to fall apart. The official report of the September 11th attacks and the increasing "war on terror" just wasn't adding up. For the first few years after the World Trade Center was destroyed, so-called "9/11 conspiracy theories" were limited to the Internet. Still, around 2005 and 2006, they proceeded into the mainstream and found many high-profile advocates whose comments about 9/11 being an "inside job" couldn't be overlooked by the mainstream media.

When individuals thinking about examining the huge disparities in the main story attempted piecing together what happened that day, it inevitably took many people "down the rabbit hole" to find the various secret societies that all led back to the Illuminati. 9/11 would lead to Skull & Bones, which would lead to the Bilderberg Group, which would cause the Bohemian Grove, which would result in the Illuminati and a whole lot of evils that raised much more questions about what the shadowy elite of the world are engaging in behind the scenes was opened.

When people take their minds off mainstream media and popular culture, step back from their self-absorbed way of life, and look deeper into world events and the power structure-directing society, they start to see the world in a very different way.

When someone starts to comprehend that there is more than meets the eye in our world and finds the different branches of elite networks that all assemble under one umbrella, their life is often never the same. People explain it as their awakening to what's occurring on the earth or "decreasing the bunny hole," or having their eyes lastly opened.

If one truly wants to learn about the world's history and the driving force behind major world events, the economy, and even our very culture, then one should check out the Illuminati. At one point in history, in the late 1700s, when the Illuminati was first exposed, many people learned about them and the threats they posed, but as time went on and generations have passed, the majority of people had ignored them. Celebrity News andSports entertainment had controlled the majority of people's minds, and a lot of people had fallen asleep, believing everything was simply outstanding.

Many people used to doubt and deny that the Italian Mafia even existed, the same holds of the modern Illuminati. Ancient secret societies are admitted by mainstream historians to have existed and were not just social clubs for men looking to keep themselves amused after work. They had a useful function, even at that time. Manly P. Hall, a respected secret society expert, explains, "The esoteric organizations of ancient times were, for the most part, philosophical and spiritual. In the medieval world, they were political and philosophical. In the modern-day world, political and social."

He goes on to explain more clearly, "It is beyond doubt that the secret societies of all ages have worked out a significant degree of political impact," which "a second purpose for secret societies was to develop a mechanism for the perpetuation from generation to generation of policies, concepts, or systems of learning, confined to a minimal group of initiated persons."

For many years, FBI director J. Edgar Hoover rejected that the La Cosa Nostra or Italian Mafia even existed. Some had the belief that the mob was blackmailing Hoover with some compromising photos of him and his partner Clyde Tolson. Still, for whatever reason, even the head of the FBI openly denied there was any such thing as an organized criminal network that had judges, lawyers, police, and other public authorities on their payroll. All the denial changed in 1957 after a crucial mafia meeting held on a farm in Apalachin, New York (about 200 miles northwest of New York City), was discovered, now understood as the Apalachin Meeting.

What are the realities, and what is fiction? How did it all begin? What is the evidence for the Illuminati's existence? What are its objectives? Are they communicating with alien beings from another galaxy that covertly work with them and guide them in their evil methods? Are they alien beings disguised as people? You will discover as you dive headfirst Inside the Illuminati.

CHAPTER ONE

Qanon Conspiracy Theory and The New World Order

QAnon might best be understood as an instance of what historian Richard Hofstadter in 1964 called "The Paranoid Style in American Politics," associated with spiritual millenarianism and apocalypticism. The vocabulary of QAnon mirrors Christian tropes--" The Storm" (the Genesis flooding narrative or Judgement Day) and "The Great Awakening," which evokes the historic spiritual Great Awakenings from the very early 18th century to the late 20th century. According to one QAnon video, the fight between Trump and also "the cabal" is of "scriptural percents," a "fight for the planet, of wicked versus outstanding." Some QAnon states the forthcoming numeration supports a "reverse rapture," which is not merely the end of the world as it is currently understood, yet a clean slate also, with redemption and a paradise on earth for the survivors. Within less than a year of existence, QAnon came to be significantly identified by the whole populace. According to an August 2018 Qualtrics survey for The Washington Post, 58% of Floridians recognize QAnon to have a viewpoint regarding it. Of those who had a point of view, many were unwanted. Positive feelings towards QAnon were uncovered to be significantly associated with being at risk of conspiracy theory thinking. According to a March 2020 Pew study, 76% of Americans claimed they had never heard of

QAnon, 20% had listened to "a little concerning it," and 3% stated they had heard "a great a lot."

Some QAnon followers have inevitably begun to acknowledge that they have been divided from family and liked ones and experience isolation due to it. For some, this is a path to beginning the process of divesting themselves of their cultish ideas. In contrast, for others, the isolation reinforces the advantages they obtain from originating from the cult.

People in the QAnon community usually mention alienation from friends and family members. Though they typically speak regarding just how Q tore their connections on private Facebook groups. Yet they think these problems are temporary and also primarily the mistake of others. They frequently comfort themselves by visualizing that there will be a time of retribution at some point in the future, which will show their beliefs. After this occurs, they think that not just will their relationships be brought back, but individuals will depend on them as leaders who understand what's taking place better than the remaining of us.

There are many systemic conspiracy theories where the concept of a New World Order is seen. The following is a checklist of the major ones in roughly sequential order:

Freemasonry Masonic Conspiracy Theory

Freemasonry is just one of the globe's earliest nonreligious fraternal business and developed during the late 16th and early 17th century Britain. Over the years, several cases and conspiracy theories have been routed towards Freemasonry, including the claims that Freemasons have a concealed political agenda and are conspiring to cause a New World Order, a world government organized according to Masonic concepts or governed just by Freemasons. The mystical nature of Masonic importance and ceremonies resulted in Freemasons initially implicated in secretly practicing Satanism in the late 18th century. The original claims of a conspiracy theory within Freemasonry to overturn religion and governments to take control of the world traces back to Scottish writer John Robison, whose reactionary conspiracy theory concepts went across the Atlantic and influenced breakouts of Protestant anti-Masonry in the United States throughout the 19th century. In the 1890s, French writer LéoTaxil composed a series of pamphlets and books disparaging Freemasonry and billing their lodges with venerating Lucifer as the Supreme Being and Great Architect the universe. Even with the fact that Taxil confessed that his claims were all a rip-off, they were and still are believed and also repeated by many conspiracy theory philosophers and had a significant effect on succeeding anti-Masonic claims regarding Freemasonry.

Some conspiracy theory philosophers eventually assumed that some Founding Fathers of the United States, such as George Washington and Benjamin Franklin, were having Masonic spiritual geometric layouts interwoven right into American culture, particularly in the Great Seal of the United States, the United States one-dollar bill, the design of National Mall sites and the roads and highways of Washington, D.C., as a component of a master method to create the first "Masonic federal government" as a design for the coming New World Order.

A Masonic Lodge area

Freemasons rebut these claims of a Masonic conspiracy theory. Freemasonry, which advertises rationalism, places no power in occult symbols. It is not a part of its principle to see the illustration of symbols, regardless of how large, as an act of managing or consolidating power. Additionally, no published details establish the Masonic membership of the men accountable for the Great Seal design. While conspiracy philosophers assert that there are aspects of Masonic impact on the Great Seal of the United States, these components were purposefully or accidentally used, considering that the developers knew the symbols. The many Grand Lodges are independent and sovereign, recommending they act independently and do not have a common agenda. The points of belief of the numerous lodges regularly differ.

End time

In the 19th century, a lot of apocalyptic millennial Christian eschatologists, starting with John Nelson Darby, have forecasted a globalist conspiracy to impose a tyrannical New World Order, controlling structure as the fulfillment of prophecies concerning the "end time" in the Bible, specifically in the Book of Ezekiel, Daniel, the Olivet discovered in the Synoptic Gospels and the Book of Revelation. They claim that individuals who have dealt with the Devil to obtain riches and also power have become pawns in a supernatural chess game have moved humanity right into approving a utopian globe government that hinges on the spiritual frameworks of syncretic-messianic world faiths, which will in the future subject itself to be a dystopian globe empire that imposes the imperial cult of an "Unholy Trinity" of Satan, the Antichrist and also the False Prophet.

Dynamic Christians, such as preacher-theologian Peter J. Gomes, caution Christian fundamentalists that a "spirit of fear" can batter scripture and history with precariously incorporating scriptural literalism, apocalyptic timetables, demonization, and overbearing bias. In contrast, Camp cautions the danger that Christians could pick up some added spiritual baggage" by credulously accepting conspiracy concepts. They seek Christians that enjoy conspiracism to repent.

Illuminati

The Order of the Illuminati was an Enlightenment-age secret society established by Adam Weishaupt on 1 May 1776, a university professor, in Upper Bavaria, Germany. The movement include advocates of freethought, secularism, sex, liberalism, and also republicanism equal rights, hired from the German Masonic Lodges, that looked for to educate rationalism through enigma schools. In 1785, the order was penetrated, separated, and reduced by the government reps of Charles Theodore, Elector of Bavaria, in his preemptive campaign to neutralize the risk of secret societies before winding up being dens of conspiracies to topple the Bavarian monarchy and its state religious beliefs, Roman Catholicism. There is no evidence that the Bavarian Illuminati survived its reductions in 1785. In the late 18th century, reactionary conspiracy philosophers, such as Scottish physicist John Robison and French Jesuit clergyman Augustin Barruel, started hypothesizing that the Illuminati had withstood their reductions come to be the masterminds behind the French Revolution and the Reign of Terror. Throughout the 19th century, fear of an Illuminati conspiracy was a real concern of the European gentility. Their oppressive reactions to this unproven fear provoked in 1848 the changes they sought to prevent.

The Protocols of the Elders of Zion

 The Protocols of the Elders of Zion is an antisemitic canard, at first released in Russian in 1903, proclaiming a Judeo-Masonic conspiracy theory to obtain globe prominence. The message proclaims to be the minutes of the secret meetings of a cabal of Jewish masterminds, which has co-opted Freemasonry and is plotting to rule the world on all Jews because they think themselves to be the chosen people of God. The Protocols integrate many of the core conspiracist themes outlined in the Robison and Barruel assaults on the Freemasons and overlay them with antisemitic allegations about anti-Tsarist movements in Russia.

The Open Conspiracy

The Open Conspiracy British author and futurist H. G. Wells promoted cosmopolitanism and prepare blueprints for a world to establish a technocratic world state and also ready economic situation. Wells warned, nonetheless, in his 1940 book The New World Order that: when the battle seems drifting in the direction of a world social democracy, there might still be great delays and disappointments before it winds up being an efficient and beneficent world system.

Countless individuals will indeed despise the brand-new world order, be rendered disgruntled by the frustration of their enthusiasm and aspirations with its growth, and will die protesting against it. When we attempt to assess its promise, we have to bear in mind the distress of a generation or more of malcontents, countless of them graceful-looking and mostly gallant individuals. Wells's books were significant in offering the 2nd meaning to the term "new world order," which would just be used by state socialist supporters and anti-communist oppositions for generations to come.

Despite his ideas' appeal and prestige, Wells failed to work deeper because he could not concentrate his energies on a direct request to intelligentsias who would, inevitably, have to collaborate the Wellsian brand-new world order.

CHAPTER TWO

The Illuminati World

The infamous Illuminati secret society has remained the focus of so-called "conspiracy theorists" for centuries. They have been called the puppet masters who secretly pull the strings of the world's events from elections to revolutions, and from business monopolies to stock exchange crashes. A substantial variety of researchers and ordinary citizens have differing degrees of suspicion that, in some way, someplace, a secret program is continuously hiding behind the scenes.

When unexpected occurrences happen on the planet, these individuals don't see them as a random incident, but as the work of a hidden hand that has managed or encouraged these occurrences to take place for the personal, professional, or monetary gain of particular individuals. Usually, such speculation is referred to as a "conspiracy theory" and dismissed as creative thinking. Many of the world's events don't make total sense, even to the so-called specialists who study them. Something is missing out from a strong explanation. More to the story than meets the eye, but these supposed professionals are often afraid to hypothesize on what that missing piece of the puzzle is.

Individuals look at disastrous occurrences like the attacks on the World Trade Center on 9/11 and question how such a thing could happen without law enforcement and intelligence firms knowing about it. Individuals take a look at the home mortgage collapse of 2008 and the following financial consequences of bank failures and government bailouts and question how such a thing could occur. People see their standard of living going down and how they can hardly manage and question how can this be? People hear on the news that child molesters and rapists get out of jail after just a couple of years, but others are locked up for decades after getting busted with some marijuana.

So individuals turn to the television to keep their mind off such things. With the push of a button, their reason is made for relaxing with the relaxing images of seeing stunning candidates contend with being this season's American Idol, or they get an adrenaline rush as their preferred football team scores a winning touchdown with just seconds left on the clock. These things make good sense to them, and its what others will discuss the next day at work, and if they wish to feel connected with others, they have to participate in these pointless activities.

The reality of the matter is that when you step back and take a closer look at the world that we are living in and at what truly matters, at the sources of information we continuously rely on, and put together several pieces of this mysterious puzzle called life, a quite different image starts to emerge. What ought to be the top story on the news is mitigated to a little and unwary article in the back half of the paper and is entirely left out from broadcast news. What should ordinarily be in celebrity chatter publication is the top story on the significant television networks. Why does this occur?

One begins to see things much differently when discovering the concrete reality of secret societies and their influence and power. As in the last few years, when one discovers the growing trustworthy details about these secret societies, their subscription, objectives, and achievements, one sees a gaping hole in the legitimacy and precision of traditional media and general knowledge.

Any discussion of a "conspiracy" or secret agenda being performed by an organization of rich and powerful guys is generally countered with laughter by the average person who mindlessly follows the herd.

Is it that difficult to think an organization of powerful men has made a pact with each other to enhance their programs secretly? Is it that tough to design a self-perpetuating structure that would enable such an organization to continually function no matter who inhabits any one position at any time? Is it far-fetched to think that these people would buy and manage the mainstream media and utilize this useful tool to further their objectives?

One of the first truth shows ever produced was called Survivor, which began airing in May of 2000. The show featured sixteen individuals placed on a secluded island and contended for one million dollars every week; an entrant was voted off the program by their fellow castaways. As the show went on, some people on the island would secretly arrange to help each other out at the expense of others who were not part of their plan. The outsiders had no idea such an agreement was made, and when bad occurrences fell upon them, they didn't think anything aside from misfortune. However, unknown to them, they were a victim of a conspiracy—a victim of the workings of a secret society within the group of candidates.

As future seasons of Survivor were aired, the secret alliances would end up being a common theme of the show to viewers who had a watchful eye of the functions of all who were on the island. Devious contestants constantly found such an idea a reliable and practical way to get ahead.

If the development of a secret alliance among members on Survivor became a standard method of taking advantage over others and to "make it through," is it that far-fetched to believe that similar secret alliances take place in business or politics? It appears that the idea to form a secret alliance exclusively for the benefit of those involved is completely sensible, and the very best way to safeguard such an alliance and ensure its success is to prevent others who are not a part of it from becoming mindful that such a thing even exists.

We understand the fact that secret societies exist in politics, business, and faith. A lot of these associations have existed for centuries. The existence of such societies spawns speculation from outsiders, and often fear. With little information to work from to formulate a trusted theory as to what these individuals are doing and the repercussions of their actions might be, it is often hard to accurately comprehend the functions of a secret society or alliance. But just as the most careful criminal, secret societies often leave hints behind. No matter the number of preventative measures one takes to prevent any understanding of their actions, it is nearly difficult to carry out a plot flawlessly without leaving proof behind. Similar to some murder cases, the evidence might not be understood right away after the criminal offense, or it may not even be discovered as proof at all. As time passes, other hints from comparable criminal activities may emerge and shed new light on things that were initially neglected.

In regards to the Illuminati, hints have been discovered over the past several hundred years. Something is undoubtedly being kept secret by some powerful and influential individuals. A network, a plan, a source of wealth and power, a reason for the secrecy, and more. In more modern times, beginning in about the late 1970s, various people have stepped forward and claimed to be real members of this elusive group and said they had defected and turned to Christianity. These guys have stated stories declaring to expose some of the Illuminati secret society's history, beliefs, and objectives. A few of their claims appear reasonable, others stretch of the creativity, and others apparent lies. Their statement, together with any inconsistencies, will be addressed in this book.

Covered are collections of many pieces of proof about the Illuminati, consisting of initial works taken in 1786 from the homes of some of the members. These works are indeed genuine, and no scholar or historian will refute that. The only refutations are regarding whether the organization could continue its work in the years following its initial exposure to the general public, over about two hundred years earlier. When one checks out the words of creator Adam Weishaupt, it appears difficult that the organization didn't continue to exist and later prosper. Since its leadership was found, it seems somehow stupid to believe that their objectives would merely be abandoned.

Had Adam Weishaupt not created and documented such an organization's plans, it seems that another power starving diabolical would have done the same. If Thomas Edison had not invented the light bulb, surely you would not have the opportunity to read these words by candlelight. Another man would have used the power of electricity just as efficiently. Such an invention was inevitable, and other men who had no connection with Edison were working towards the same objective. Cultures worldwide throughout history that have had no contact with each other have made comparable and often similar developments and discoveries. Humanity's interests are equal worldwide, just as our ethical drawbacks are.

The very idea of a secret alliance among guys to include each other's goals at the expense of others and under a shroud of secrecy surely isn't a unique idea. Mafias and arranged criminal businesses have sprung up worldwide and have similar structures and approaches, but another has influenced few.

The idea of a secret group that has vowed allegiance to each other over all others need to be as significant to our lives as falling in love. And just as this human condition of interpersonal relationships has ended up being a classic theme in Hollywood motion pictures, we ought to think that a similar style would be found too, and it is. A deceptive group of bad people who outline greed, destruction, or harm.

While a range of traditional Hollywood stories continues to be produced, with a number of them involving secret criminal alliances, it is interesting that an uncommon variety of them will integrate plots very comparable to occurrences in reality associated with the functions of the Illuminati.

Even more unusual, the name "Illuminati" is used to explain the group that is behind the events in these films. After analyzing Illuminati themes, symbolism, and recommendations in popular Hollywood films, one can arrive at no other conclusion than the writers and producers of those movies have a detailed understanding of the Illuminati itself.

While they are not producing a documentary film attempting to expose the company like the different ones discussed in this book, one can't help but think that they are trying to get across to the audience in a similar method. After all, one can learn a lesson from reading the facts or hearing a story about such events in a fable or allegory.

Much like Aesop's fables include underlying ethical messages conveyed through made-up words. A few of these Hollywood films' themes consist of plotlines surrounding terrorism, mind control, Big Brother, secret societies, and occult mysticism and magic.

While some uninformed skeptics believe that when someone discusses the Illuminati, they got the idea from a Hollywood movie, the reverse is true. Many writers and producers have gotten their ideas from the accurate and historic Illuminati.

In October of 1963, a man named Joe Valachi testified before the McClellan Congressional Committee on organized criminal activity where he informed the authorities about the Italian Mafia's inner workings and how significant their organization was. He described how they controlled a market selection and had cops and judges in their pockets from either dangers or rewards. The story was too unique for the authorities when Valachi was first taken into custody and began informing the police about the Mafia. They could not comprehend how a secret criminal business could be useful and operate without notice in so many social sectors. Valachi was locked away in a mental medical facility and was believed to be outrageous. Just later, did authorities recognize he was telling the truth, and as La Cosa Nostra was uncovered, their criminal empire's level started to be comprehended.

The topic of "the Mafia" continues to fascinate people. If one didn't understand their history, they might think that well known Hollywood films such as Goodfellas and Casino are entirely fictional, but are based on true stories. The gangsters represented in these films did live lives of high-end and fantastic influence. They were also callous killers.

One can't help but discover the deafening and odd silence on specific issues by so-called experts in the mainstream media. How is it that Rush Limbaugh, Sean Hannity, Alan Colmes, Bill O'Reilly, and others disregard concerns surrounding the Illuminati every year? Problems with tangible, strong evidence that is undeniable. For instance, the annual Bilderberg conference or the Cremation of Care event at the Bohemian Grove or the Federal Reserve Bank's dedicated functions. Surely these are at least fascinating enough stories for a periodic section. Still, for years, these so-called political professionals and analysts inexplicably omit any mention of such problems and organizations from their shows.

The response is that the majority of these people know much about these concerns. A lot of them are accomplices and individuals in such things.

These individuals are paid millions of dollars a year to captivate the general public with problems of little significance and to set the program of the public state of mind in a manner that excludes any genuine responses to what is at stake and what is occurring in Washington. These propagandists parrot talking points that are offered to them daily by the people who sign their paychecks and choose to act as gate-keepers whenever a delicate concern might be dealt with. These talking heads can't plead ignorance because they are often a part of the inner circle they protect. Even during call-in radio talk shows, when the format is relaxed, and the hosts inform the audience that "any subject is fair game," they do not mean what they say. Any pertinent concern that falls beyond the recommended paradigm they are perpetuating faces the call screener. If it makes it on the airwaves, the caller gets hung up immediately, and their question is either ridiculed or overlooked.

Some essential gamers in settings of power and influence might not be a participant, and even mindful that they are serving the Illuminati, or that the culture exists in all. These people perform an egotistical plan to benefit those who have guaranteed them rewards in return or progress for their participation.

While these gamers recognize that they are a component of a private or deceptive agreement pushing an agenda, many do not acknowledge that they are a pawn in a bigger conspiracy. Their only objectives are power, status, and money. A few of their activities are criminal, and some have been caught as well as imprisoned. The basic reason is that many prepared servants go along with Illuminati schemes while not seeing the underlying forces directing a larger operation.

Knowledge or Information is power, and the Illuminati know this. Having accessibility to accurate and reliable information is indeed power, and the capacity to dispense false and misleading information is additional power. As one reads words of the initial writings of the Illuminati, one finds that the beginning participants recognized this in the late 1700s, long before the communication age. By taking over the mainstream media in all forms as it created, television, print, and also radio, they have been able to contain information and also dispense deceptive or pointless stories to the public.

If the people did not see it on CNN or Fox News, they have not to be taking place, they assume. It has only been with publications released by small independent authors. In the later years of the Internet's arrival, it has allowed those that are hungry to find something substantial to please their wishes. Web sites like Infowars.com and, to a lower degree, DrudgeReport.com have let us bypass the monopoly control of information given by the mainstream media.

In compliance with web pages, this author has compiled both details from the original works of the Illuminati and a few of the first writers to create publications exposing them and their objectives, in addition to one of the most exact writers and researchers who have continued that tradition. You will find the testament of women and men who either asserted to have been Illuminati members or victims of some of its members. You will additionally find a compilation of the uncommon circumstances that Illuminati associated topics are discussed or alluded to in mainstream media sources.

Many suspected or confirmed Illuminati created and controlled class of organizations are rarely pointed out in the mainstream information. These one-of-a-kind occurrences have been put together in this book.

Finally, you will find a summary of several references, both indirect and direct, to the Illuminati and their activities that are found in prominent Hollywood movies, books, and television shows. Such rare mentions go undetected by visitors unaware of the deeper meanings that these storylines and personalities have.

With bits and items of dependable details regarding some fairly popular secret societies and organizations like the Skull and Bones society, the Bohemian Grove, and the Bilderberg team being launched to the public, we have concrete evidence those who are involved with such organizations. Authentic subscription lists have been taken or otherwise obtained from the Bohemian Grove, and visitor listings have been gotten incomparable fashion concerning Bilderberg guests. Sometimes, as with President George W. Bush and Senator John Kerry, men have publicly confessed being members of Skull and Bones, but rejected any comment beyond that. We have a clear suggestion of who is included in such an organization. We can see by their résumés that they have achieved personal, economic, and political success far beyond various other competitors. It would certainly be crazy not to see a clear pattern in all of this.

These secret societies, organizations, and meetings exist. This is beyond a doubt and with mountains of undeniable proof to sustain this type of conclusion. They live for an objective they have existed for centuries. Their existence and purpose exceed a plain social gathering, as alcohol, parties and dinners are for.

After reading all the evidence, one must reasonably conclude that they exist partially to improve each other's occupations using secret alliances. One has a better idea of just how the political landscape is created when this is realized. There is also a more extensive program that is being carried out and is directed by those at greater levels of power within the Illuminati. A satanic and occulticschedule is sustaining the New World Order's building and the organized slavery of the human race.

Suppose this level of understanding is gotten to by an outsider. In that case, it is just the outcome of their standard being tested after discovering the truth of mysticism and occult philosophies and rituals that are part of most of these organizations.

It is one thing to observe and understand secret alliances among the rich and powerful implied for their personal and professional enhancement. It is something entirely different to see these alliances in the context of fancy and unusual hellish routines, as in the initiation into the Skull and Bones society, or the yearly Cremation of Care ritual in the secluded redwood forest of the Bohemian Grove.

These are established men we are discussing about. One of the most innovative, informed, and wealthy men on the planet from famous households, but they take part in such things. Initially, it appears so improbable that it is reasonable to easily reject such accusations as extravagant rumors or the ramblings of a mentally insane individual. The closer one looks right into these points; the more irrefutable such claims come to be.

One who ponders these issues also inevitably comes to the question of the Illuminati's ultimate purpose? Why is there a need to create the New World Order global government? What then? What role do the occult rituals and necromancies play in all of this? The solutions are located both in Bible prophecy and also within the teachings of the occult as well as New Age organizations. They parallel each other entirely to their verdicts, at which point they substantially differ.

New Age and occult teachings predict that when the New World Order facilities and ideologies are complete, from within the hierarchy of the Illuminati will indeed arrive the long-expected and awaited messiah. They believe that he will undoubtedly unify all the world's religious beliefs into one compatible formula, and the fact that he will fulfill all predictions of the coming savior of the world. They also say that, at the moment, the secret hierarchy of well-informed masters will be able to appear from the shadows in what is called the externalization of the order, and afterward, finally reveal themselves to the world and disclose the surprising wisdom that they had kept protected for many generations.

The appearance of this New Age Christ will then eliminate all discomfort and struggle with the world. All poverty and sickness, all prejudice as well as criminal offense. All lacks as well as shortage, all worries, as well as stress and anxiety. It is at this point that the world and all that populate it will ultimately have the ability to stay in perfect peace and consistency with each other, many thanks to the revelations of this Illuminati messiah and the hierarchy.

They needed to work in secret and deny their presence for hundreds of years, to secure themselves from their opponents. It is only now that their very great work is completed that they may lastly expose themselves with no anxiety of consequences. This is all, according to the teachings in New Age enlightenment circles and occultic hierarchy. These teachings report that this Illuminati Christ will be a super-human demigod or perhaps a being from one more planet or dimension.

On the other hand, according to Christianity, Islam, and various other religions, the New World Order global realm will be taken control of by the Antichrist and his followers. In this sight, a man will additionally claim to be the world's messiah and hold the trick to fixing humankind's problems. Only in this view, the core of humanity's troubles include those who disagree that he is the messiah. The freedom from prejudice that he promises is impeded by Christians and others that see him as a fake Christ and the Antichrist. The perversions and immorality that he is preaching are resisted and denounced by faithful Christians that see such habits as sinful and socially and spiritually destructive.

Equally, As Adolf Hitler guaranteed tranquility and financial success in Germany once the Jews were gotten rid of, the Antichrist will use the same remedy and single out the resistant Christians and others as the challenge to peace and prosperity. These old made Christians with their outdated customs and beliefs hold back the unity of humanity; the Antichrist will inform the world. Individuals who still believe in personal property, individual privacy, and the concepts set out in the United States' initial Constitution are the ones who are disrupting the new system. Those that will decline implantable integrated circuits and tracking tools or neural interfaces wired directly into their minds. Those who talk out against such things are the individuals who need to be eliminated for there to be peace. This, obviously, according to the Illuminati messiah and his advocates.

At some point throughout this challenge, Christians think that Jesus will go back to the planet, and the Apocalypse will take place, exposing the fake Christ and also casting him right into Hell. God is stated to ultimately introduce the enigmas of existence and life's struggles and damage or punish those who did not follow his rules. Those faithful to God's ideas will then be permanently awarded for their nonpartisanship and guts

Pre Illuminati Organizations.

Many of the information dispersed about the Illuminati comes from the Knights Templar, the Freemasons, and the Bavarian Illuminati established in Germany in 1776. It's crucial to keep in mind that nearly the same kind of organization had existed previously, for hundreds of years. The Knights Templar date back to the 1100s and the Freemasons to the late 1500s, but before these organizations had developed, secret cultures which possessed supposed underground expertise had existed much previously. It would later turn into these newer and much more advanced groups.

Expertise has usually provided power, and dating back to old Egypt as well as Greece, groups of men had maintained expertise to themselves and only exposed it to others in incremental degrees within what was called the Mysteries, or the Mystery institutions. As medicine, art, and research were progressing and new explorations were being made, the adepts or beginning of these Mystery schools were the ones on the cutting side. These organizations were often comprised of the brightest guys.

The Mystery schools served as a strategy for spiritual enlightenment as well. Mystical and spiritual theories were shown and acted out in routines and events to communicate symbolic significance to the initiates. While these Mystery colleges might not have helped in any bad intentions or plotted any wicked plans against non-members and society all at once, one can comprehend how launches in the Mysteries might establish a superiority complex and use the cover of the organizations to assist them in performing their professional and political programs. Some believe that the Mystery schools once had the highest possible standards relating to the personality and stability of the members, and they were slowly damaged, and such virtues were replaced with selfishness as well as wickedness.

CHAPTER THREE

The Luciferian Doctrine and the Dark Agenda

It is obvious from the works of famous Freemasons and Illuminati authors that the elite members' religious beliefs and approach are that of Satanism or Luciferianism. Whether this is a literal belief or a symbolic or a metaphoric belief is of little difference. It would then be metaphoric as well if it were literal. If it were metaphoric, it additionally increases into a literal style as the participants' activities materialize themselves.

To sum up, Satanism or Luciferianismone must comprehend the distinction between theistic Satanism and atheistic Satanism.

Atheistic Satanism was popularized in the late 1960s by Anton LaVey, the creator of the Church of Satan, and also the writer of The Satanic Bible. While misleading and complicated, he and his followers profess that they are atheists and don't believe in a literal Devil, and even God. They don't rely on an afterlife or a Heaven or Hell, either. These individuals prefer to call themselves Satanists and use the symbol of Satan for its rebellious and nonconformist undertones.

Theistic Satanism, on the other hand, is the belief in a God and a Devil, as well as superordinary beings. These Satanists take the opposite side of the Christian perception concerning the Garden of Eden and the Fall of Man. In Christianity and Judaism, the book of Genesis defines how God created Adam and Eve as well as how they lived in the Garden of Eden. God was claimed to have informed them that they were not to eat the forbidden fruit from a specified tree of knowledge of good and evil, for if they did, they would certainly pass away.

As the story goes, Satan showed up to Eve as a serpent and attracted her to eat the fruit. Genesis 3:1 -7 states; "The woman started to the snake, "we might eat fruit from the trees in the garden, yet God said, 'You shall not eat fruit from the tree that is in the middle of the garden, and you shall not touch it, or you will die.'".

" You will certainly not die," the serpent stated to the woman. "For God knows the fact that when you eat of the fruit, your eyes will be opened, and you will certainly be like God, understanding evil and good.".

" When the woman saw that the fruit of the said tree was great for food as well as pleasing to the eye, and additionally desirable for gaining knowledge, she eventually took some and ate it. She later offered some to her husband, who was actually with her, and he also consumed it. The eyes of both of them were opened, and they found out they were naked, so they went ahead to sew fig leaves together and made coverings for themselves.".

Theistic Satanists and Luciferians believe that Satan came to the Garden of Eden to save Adam and Eve and humankind from ignorance, and that God didn't want them to have the understanding since, then they would not be his slaves. In this way, God is viewed as the oppressor and the bad one, while Satan is viewed as the hero and savior. This is why in such publications as The Secret Doctrine, author Helena Blavatsky refers to Satan as the holy spirit.

She wrote in the book, "Thus "SATAN," once he ceases to be viewed in the dogmatic, superstitious, unphilosophical spirit of the Churches, grows into the glorious image of someone who made from terrestrial a divine MAN; who offered him, throughout the long cycle of Maha-Kalpa the law of the Spirit of Life, as well as made him free from the Sin of Ignorance.".

"The real meaning is even more philosophical, as well as the legend of the first "Fall" (of the angels) takes a scientific coloring when adequately understood."

This is among the reasons the Illuminati has a hierarchical structure, and only gives knowledge gradually as members climb the ranks. Indeed, knowledge is power, and they have taken the fruit from the tree of knowledge of good and evil. They have hidden it away, making use of it as a carrot to attract lower degree initiates to do the organization's bidding so that they may be well awarded with not just their social and financial assistance, but with the prohibited occult knowledge of Man's past and of the nature of truth itself. Such prohibited knowledge, they think, holds the potential for a man to come to be god-like.

The term Lucifer, being synonymous with Satan, is Latin for "light-bearer," which is the reason Satanists and Luciferians believe that the Devil is the source of wisdom and knowledge. Thus he is excellent. While in Christianity, Jesus is claimed to be the light of the world, the Illuminati direct this quality to Satan or Lucifer. Satan's name implies "opponent" or accuser and is, for that reason, the enemy of God. Satan is given the title of Lucifer simply because he brings the forbidden wisdom or knowledge that God did not want humanity to have, In Christianity and Luciferianism and various other religions, the term "light" stands for love, wisdom, and knowledge. One primary difference between a lot of faiths and Luciferianism is that Christianity and most religions freely educate their message and welcome everyone to discover it and comprehend it, where occultism keeps its message hidden from the majority of people and doesn't share its expertise with others.

The word occult implies "concealed." The primary distinction between Luciferianism and Christianity is that traditional Christianity teaches that salvation comes just by believing in Jesus, where sorcerers believe that one is saved by learning the secret understanding. While this idea of salvation by knowledge is not overtly wicked and sinister, it is what the Illuminati have done with this concept that shows they are a cabal of hypocrites, liars, and tyrants.

The term Illuminati is Latin for Illuminated ones and is additionally a reference to light, brilliance, and Lucifer.

Inside the Mindset of the Illuminati.

When one completely comprehends the religion of the Illuminati and its subsidiary branches such as high-level Freemasons, Skull and Bones members, as well as attendees of Bohemian Grove, one can battle it out with the reality of this Luciferian doctrine. While several openly known organizations such as the Freemason pride themselves on getting their members instilled with moral character, how come these elite members can be Satan adorers? Do they know the truth? Is

Satan truly the good god, and the God of the Bible is the wicked one holding knowledge, wisdom, and blessings back from the human race?

If the Illuminati possess the truth about the history of our creation, existence, and God's nature, then are they betraying their own god by keeping that truth, wisdom, and knowledge from others? What about not just keeping that said truth from people, but actually lying to them, or ruthlessly taking advantage of other people or stealing what belongs to them? Whatever they believe the truth is, they are keeping it to themselves and putting out a continuous stream of propaganda, out-right lies, and disinformation, just to protect against others discovering that truth.

While almost every religion on earth from Christianity, to Islam, to Buddhism and Hinduism, wants every person to understand what they consider to be the truth, it is the Illuminati that do not comply with these ideals. Elite members do not adhere to the principle of life, treating others the way you intend to be treated. Instead, they violate virtually every significant values found in faiths or religions around the globe. Please do not lie, do not swipe, do not murder, do not fancy; these rules mean nothing to the Illuminati and its subsidiary organizations' elite members.

These revelations commonly result in whether these people count on an afterlife or a judgment from God after they pass away. Many religious beliefs think that they will undoubtedly stand before God and face sentences for their transgressions when one passes away. Under this form of belief system, even if a person survives life without being caught for their transgressions, they will one day pay the afterlife price in a purgatory for short-lived punishment or burning in Hell forever.

As a result, one wonders what the Illuminati believe will happen to them when they die. Just how will they escape Divine justice for all of their misdeeds?

There are two explanations for this. One is that they do not believe in an afterlife, that we are just sophisticated animals having no soul, and when we are dead, there is no afterlife, nor judgment. This explains their social Darwinist world view and their unreasonable parasitic techniques, which eventually robs others of their sanity, money, health, and freedom. Another necessary explanation is that the Illuminati believe that God does not judge us personally, but in an impersonal fashion based on a scale of good deeds versus evil acts. In this sight, one is thought to be able to cancel their Karma, in a manner of speaking, as well as stay clear of any type of undesirable effects for their indiscretions.

Both of these explanations bring about other questions. Is the Illuminati, right? Are we merely animals without soul or afterlife? If we are religious, are we the ones living a lie? For argument's purpose, they are right that there is no immortality and no judgment from God after one dies. Even if it holds, if most of us were to obey their philosophy, then our society would undoubtedly be a dangerous place, meaningless and unfulfilling. Life would be Hell on earth if every man were out for himself, and we all would break the necessary moral code of the civilized world. If there is no immortality or judgment from God, no Heaven or Hell, then the short life that we live on this world would still be more pleasurable, fulfilling, as well as safe if we were to live by Biblical principles than if we were to obey the Illuminati's code of do what thou wants.

The Illuminati might have the whole truth, or they may have just a piece of it and assume they have it all as a whole, like a blind guy who gets hold of an elephant's tail and thinks that it is an elephant, not recognizing he is only holding a tiny part of an elephant and can not begin to picture what an elephant is, based upon the small part that he is holding in his hand.

Regardless of their supposed exceptional wisdom and knowledge, the Illuminati have been wrong in the past. They have been blinded by their pride and intoxicated from their power. Adolf Hitler, together with his elite inner circle of Nazis, thought that they would rule the world and build a new race of enlightened super-men. They thought that magical powers were on their side, and their destiny was to build a thousand-year empire with Adolf Hitler as its high priest. Instead, their strategies fell apart as Hitler and his closest allies were compelled to commit suicide in defeat.

In philosophy, a concept called Pascal's wager suggests that if one were to live as though there was no God or final judgment, and they were incorrect, they would have a significant loss. But if somebody were to live as though there is a God, and God has established rules for us to comply with, which each individual will be rewarded or punished for their acts, then if they turn out to be wrong, they would have lost nothing and would have had a much safer and more fulfilling life anyway. Pascal suggested that even though we can not prove God's true existence through scientific inquiry or reason, people should wager as though he exists because one has potentially everything to gain and nothing to lose by doing so.

While learning the details of occult philosophy can cause one to wrestle with their faith, one must know there are real consequences to how we chose to live our lives.

Whatever one's faith is, a universal code of conductin the world exists. It is clear that the Illuminati consistently breaks that code while providing the society with a false face that they abide by the same rules everyone else is required to follow.

CHAPTER FOUR

The Edicts

The 1st Edict Against the Illuminati

A mandate can be referred to as an act of law made by a monarchy (just like an executive order made by a president today). On June 22, 1784, Duke Karl Theodore, the Elector of Bavaria, made the first order against the Illuminati after his sister-in-law Duchess Dowager Maria Anna was given some documents an early defector called Joseph Schneider, and then passed them onto the Duke.

The proclamation reads, in part, "Whereas all communities, societies, and associations without approval from a public authority and the confirmation of the Monarch are illegal, prohibited by law, suspect and dangerous things in [and] of themselves. His Electoral Highness [the Duke] has decided not to tolerate them in his State, whatever their designation and interior constitutions, ordering categorically ... one and all subjects to withdraw from any association or secret assembly of this kind ... those societies [have] drawn the attention of the public and awakened its fears ..."

The 2nd Edict Against the Illuminati.

In 1785, Duke Karl Theodore issued a second proclamation, which was a lot more threatening and particularly named the Illuminati and Freemasonry as the wrongdoers with a conspiracy against the government. In this order, the Duke also revealed that if anyone were to come forward and reveal who was included or specifically which masonic lodges had been infiltrated and were being used in this conspiracy-- that informant might remain confidential and even keep half the cash that was seized as a result of their confession. The other half [of the money], the proclamation stated, would be offered to the poor.

It reads in part, "We [the government] ... have been deeply impacted and displeased to learn that the different Lodges of so-called Freemasons and Illuminati, who are still in our States, have taken so little hearken of our General Prohibition released on June 22nd of last year against all fraternal societies clandestine and unapproved, as not only to continue to convene in secret, but to raise funds, and to recruit new members, seeking to boost the currently large numbers of adepts further."

The proclamation continues, "We had deemed this society, very much degenerated and of primitive organization, too suspect, both as regards to spiritual issues and from a social and political point of view, so that we could no longer tolerate it in our States ... we command that all authorities should execute our orders exactly and privately notify us of any disobedience. We state that all cash and any funds collected illegally [by the lodges] will be seized [and] half will be provided to the poor. In contrast, the other half will go to the denunciator [informant], even if he is a member of one of those societies, with a guarantee to keep his name confidential."

It concludes, "We hope that each of our subjects value enough of our favor and his honor and happiness so that all over we can count on due obedience to our orders and be excused from needing to take more serious steps."

The 3rd Edict Against the Illuminati.

On August 16, 1787, not long after the castle of Baron de Bassus was searched, where more documents were discovered, the 3rd edict against the Illuminati was made by the Duke of Bavaria saying the penalty would be death for any Illuminati member found meeting or hiring anybody to join them. "Any so charged and condemned are to be denied of their lives by the sword, while those thus hired are to have their items confiscated and themselves to be condemned to continuous banishment from the areas of the Duke. Under the same penalties of confiscation and banishment, the members of the order, no matter under what name or circumstances, irregular or regular, they should gather, are forbidden to assemble as lodges."

" As more time passes, it is further realized how harmful and dangerous the Order of the Illuminati will be for the State and religion is allowed to flourish here and beyond. It is difficult to predict the deplorable effects of posterity if we stand back, if not dealt with very seriously. At the same time, there is still time to forcefully get rid of a disease, which is far more daunting than the plague itself.".

" ... for the recruiter, he is to be deprived of life by the sword, and for the hired, he will be sentenced to have his property seized and eliminated for life from all States of His Electoral Highness, with a guarantee of never being allowed to return. Under the same penalties of forfeiture and expulsion, the prohibited Lodges of the Illuminati, under whatever name they might conceal and carefully present themselves, in all locations, must be subject to strenuous security. Those in lodge clothes will be held and dealt with as if they had attended meetings secretly, in suspect places such as hotels or specific homes. We will not permit the baseless excuses usually offered-- an open society of good friends-- specifically when those present have now been suspected of impiety and Illuminism."

The 4th Edict Against the Illuminati.

Many mainstream sources (including the frequently incorrect and unreliable Wikipedia) declare that shortly after the 3rd order was issued in 1787, the Illuminati was entirely irradiated and wasn't much of a concern after that. The issue is-- the Duke of Bavaria issued a 4th edict a couple of years later in 1790 saying that the Illuminati was not only still active but were continuing to hire new members!

On November 15, 1790, the following announcement against the Illuminati was issued by the Duke, stating, "The Elector has learned, partly by the spontaneous confession of some members, partly by sound intelligence, that despite the Edicts of July 14, 1784 and August 16th 1785 (and in the very same month in 1787), the Illuminati still hold, albeit in smaller numbers, secret meetings through the Electorate, but particularly in Munich and the surrounding area; they continue to attract boys to the cause and have maintained a correspondence with [secret] societies and with members in other countries.".

It goes on, "They continue to assault the State and especially religion, either verbally or through handouts ... Every speech, every printed book or manuscript against religion and the state need to be reported to the authorities or the Elector [Duke] himself, as well as any secret meetings. Those who have remained quiet on these problems, having undoubtedly been shown to have possessed information, will be severely punished.

The denunciator, even if he was an accessory to the crime, will receive a cash reward, and his identity will be kept confidential.".

The 4th order cautions, "Any member who has assisted in a secret meeting, has hired new members or referred [secret] societies or brothers in other countries, will be mercilessly punished by death. Any civil servant or [those in the] military, any holder of a beneficial workplace, a parish priest, and so on, must swear that he has not and will never be a part of the sector they'll be convicted of perjury and shall be penalized accordingly.".

Taking Over the Government.

One of the original Illuminati defectors called Joseph von Utschneider, who provided a deposition to the court about the Illuminati strategies, alerted that they prepared to "present an around the world ethical regime which would be under their control in every nation. This council would decide on all matters concerning promotions, appointments, and pardons, in addition to rejections ... This would give it the limitless right to pronounce last judgment over the sincerity and effectiveness of an individual.".

The confiscated correspondence between members of the group confirms this accusation. One of the letters reads, "The Order needs to have the power of life and death in consequence of our oath; and with propriety, for the same reason, and by the same right, that any government in the world possesses it.

-- for the Order comes in their place, making them unnecessary. When things can not be otherwise, and ruin would occur if the association did not use this means, the Order must, as well as public rulers, employ it for the good of humanity; therefore, for its preservation."

Several letters revealed their intent to deceive people to "guarantee their happiness."Weishaupt's megalomaniacal objectives of world domination became very clear with such declarations as, "the Order will, for its own sake, and therefore certainly, place every man in that circumstance in which he can be most efficient. The pupils are convinced that the Order will rule the world. Every member therefore becomes a ruler.".

"The great strength of our Order lies in its concealment; let it never appear in any location in its name, but constantly covered by another name, and another profession." This has successfully occurred with private organizations like the Council on Foreign Relations, the Bilderberg Group, and the Federal Reserve, taking over society's key power centers. It must be pointed out that the Founding Fathers of America documented their grievances with the Monarch in the Declaration of Independence, and 56 men signed their names to it and sent it off to the king of England. They didn't hide their objectives or trick people hoping to further their objectives. Unlike Weishaupt and the Illuminati, they were honest and open about their beliefs, strategies, and goals, who used deception and fraud as a standard practice.

Similarly, when theologian Martin Luther opposed the Catholic Church's oppressive control over 250 years before Weishaupt, he made a note of his complaints. He nailed them on the front door of his regional church in 1517. He didn't deceive or lie to anybody about his hopes of breaking the Catholic Church's stranglehold on society. Still, fellow German, Adam Weishaupt, was power-hungry himself. Rather than wanting to free society from the tyranny of the Jesuits and the Catholic Church, he wanted to be the tyrant himself.

CHAPTER FIVE

The Thirteen Bloodlines Theory

In some cases, people refer to the "Illuminati families" or the 'leading thirteen bloodlines of the Illuminati" as the ruling elite within the pyramid of power that regulates our world. A few names are thrown around and claimed to be Illuminati families that interbreed to retain their broad range power amongst the little group of the ruling elite. Some of the most common affirmed thirteen families are: Astor, Bundy, Collins, DuPont, Freeman, Kennedy, Li, Onassis, Rockefeller, Rothschild, Russell, Van Duyn, and the Merovingian bloodline.

Among the much more popular promoters of this theory is FritSpringmeier, that in 1999 released Bloodlines of the Illuminati, where he wrote, "The goal of this publication is to lay out the historic truths concerning these elite families ... as soon as one recognizes these families, the battle between kings no longer look like battles between elite intrigues, but often can be recognized as contrived battles created to control the masses of both sides by their hoggish Machiavellian masters."

Springmeier continues, "The Illuminati themselves decided to boost thirteen bloodlines. The number 13 is very crucial amazingly, and these 13 occult individuals mock the 13 tribes of Israel (remember the 13th people, the Tribe of Joseph was split right into Ephraim & Manasseh). This does not imply that just

13 Illuminati families are influential. Various other families have risen to prominence.

Further, worldwide there are other families of excellent oligarchical power that have allied themselves to the Illuminati in the financial and political realms without needing to intermarry right into the Illuminati."

While Frit]'s publication shows up externally to be an excellent evaluation of the intended thirteen bloodlines, it is clear that he bought right into some known scams and reprinted them as truth, such as the commonly unmasked claims of John Todd, a man who in the 1970s claimed to be an Illuminati "defector" coming from among the "Illuminati families."Springmeier also declares that the Illuminati have been running a spaceport station on Mars, which he claims they started colonizing in the late 1990s.

A lot more reliable scientist, Antony Sutton, who was given a Skull & Bones membership listing in the early 1980s by the daughter of a member, has a far more sensible and precise strategy. In his exceptional evaluation, America's Secret Establishment, Sutton has specified that twenty to thirty families have controlled the Skull & Bones society since its creation in 1832. His publication offers a scholarly overview of their tasks.

The thirteen family theory is a more contemporary variation of the old "divine right of kings theory, which was bolstered for thousands of years, declaring that God ordained households of kings and majesties to rule. Frequently, as with Egyptian Pharaohs, the Caesars of Rome, and the Chinese Dynasties, kings believed (or at the very least asserted to believe) that they were Gods or literal descendants of the Gods, which consequently, they thought, offered them the divine right to rule. This is not just an old idea. The Nazi's thought that white individuals were the offspring from the (supposed) God-like inhabitants of the Lost City of Atlantis.

Adolf Hitler and his internal circle of Nazi officers, consisting of Heinrich Himmler, Rudolph Hess, and Joseph Goebbels, literally believed that white people (the Aryan race, as they usually call them) were descendants of Gods that once lived in the Earth, that lived in the City of Atlantis. The Nazis assumed the misconception of the "Lost City" was a literal background. According to their ideas, when the city supposedly sunk into the sea, many of the demigods got away to the Himalayas of Tibet, where they were said to have started the Aryan and nordic races.

According to the Nazi view, the Jews, claiming to be "God's chosen people," were preventing the Aryans from their "divine right" to rule the earth, and race-mixing was weakening the enchanting power of the Aryan race. Hitler was influenced mainly by Helena Blavatsky's 1888 publication, The Secret

Doctrine, which asserts that Satan helped to free Man in the Garden of Eden, allowing human beings to "develop" right into gods themselves. "Satan will now be revealed, in the teaching of the Secret Doctrine, allegorized as Good, and Sacrifice, a God of Wisdom," the book reads, "Blessed and sanctified is the name of the Angel of Havas-- Satan," Blavatsky wrote.

Mainstream historians concentrate on the racial facets of the Nazis Test for power. However, they usually ignore the root of their ideological background, which was a twisted occult doctrine and essentially based upon Satanism and the idea that they had divine blood in their blood vessels and were descendants of gods. A German secret society called the Thule Society offered birth to the Nazi event. It ran just like the Skull & Bones society does in America, working on grooming the nation's future leaders. The Thule Society's logo was a swastika with a blade before it.

The "most imperial candidate" theory is the idea that every presidential election in the United States has been won by the candidate with the most royal blood, thus having the closest connections to the kingship bloodline of Europe.

Proponents of the theory claim that every U.S. president since George Washington can have their family traced back to European royals, and claim that thirty-three head of states are offspring of Alfred the Great and Charlemagne.

However, this pleads the Question of why a small group of families would certainly consider themselves to have "imperial blood." What does "imperial blood" mean? Well, it implies that they think they are straight offspring of the Gods. Individuals who agree with this theory usually point to a passage in the Book of Genesis in the Bible as proof. (Genesis 6:1-2) "And it came to pass, when men began to multiply on the face of the earth, and daughters were birthed unto them, That the children of God saw the daughters of man, that they were fair; and they made them wives of all which they selected." Genesis 6:4 proceeds, "There were giants in the earth in those days; and additionally after that, when the sons of God came in unto the daughters of man, and they bare children to them, the same ended up being magnificent men which were of old, men of renown.".

Some Christians and Biblical scholars believe that the "Sons of God," which came and took the children of men and had children with them, were an alien race called the Annunaki. Some versions of the Bible claim that the Sons of God were "superordinary beings" and clearly describes some type of unusual creatures that involved the planet and mated with human females, creating some sort of alien/human crossbreed called the Nephilim.

Some believe that God caused the flood wishing to destroy these Nephilim creatures and afterward have Noah, his sons. Their wives later repopulate the earth after they arise securely from

66

the Ark. According to some beliefs, those intended crossbreed creatures went and endured on to become the very first kings and queens, and later on developed into what we describe as the Illuminati today.

The misconception that Jesus Christ covertly had a child with Mary Magdalene was brought into the mainstream with Dan Brown's 2003 publication The Da Vinci Code, which was influenced by the commonly unmasked Holy Blood, HolyGrail (1982). Dan Brown's book was made right into a movie in 2006 starring Tom Hanks, which lugged the suggestion to a much bigger target market that believed the scam of the "Jesus family.".

According to the myth, the Knights Templar and Freemasons are the Holy Grail's guardians, which according to this theory, the Grail describes the descendants of Jesus and Mary Magdalene. Thus the "Holy Grail" is the divine family. Their supposed members have to stay in secret to shield themselves from being eliminated by the Catholic Church, which presumably will do anything to avoid this "secret reality" from being understood because it would undoubtedly undermine their power.

This Jesus bloodline misconception may very well be introduced eventually in time as "evidence" of the Illuminati's supposed "divine right to rule" by claiming they are the actual offspring of Jesus. It might effectively end with the look of the antichrist, who will declare to be the long-awaited messiah of the world and cite his supposed genetic connection to Jesus as evidence that he is the return of Christ.

When exploring the supposed "families of the Illuminati," you will commonly come across people speaking regarding "the Reptilians" that believe the Illuminati are essentially a group of "form moving extraterrestrials" or demonic inter-dimensional entities masquerading as humans to work towards confining the human race. The "Reptilian" concept is extensively ridiculed, although a sizable portion of the population does not doubt that renowned political leaders and stars are "impostors," only acting to be human.

Many of the Reptilian claims are straight out of the X- Files, the popular paranormal thriller from the 1990s. They are practically similar to the plot of a 1980s mini collection titled V (for visitors).

A British conspiracy philosopher named David Icke is mainly responsible for spreading this concept and claims these "Reptillian Illuminati" need to consume human blood, "since they are consuming the person's life-force and since they require it to exist in this dimension in a human form."

More lately, Icke seems to have distanced himself from "Reptlillians" and started concentrating on the Archons, which refer to supernatural representatives of the wicked Gnostic maker God, the Demiurge. Icke is also a big proponent that these "Reptillian Illuminati" families have interbred with each other throughout history to keep their unique family and conceal their trick from outsiders.

It was relatively easy to regulate who would marry whom and maintain imperial family members reproducing with other royal families in old times. The majority of people married others in the same socioeconomic level because they run in the same circles, go to the same prestigious colleges, and grow up in the same affluent areas. While the ancient alien/Nephilim bloodline theory is interesting on its surface area, there is little to no proof that people from these supposed royal or divine/alien/reptilian families have any kind of significant difference in their DNA from "normal" people or "citizens" as we are called.

In more modern times, the law of who marries whom through arranged marital relationships has become nearly impossible to control, so if this concept were real, then the "alien" DNA would undoubtedly be so commonly spread that we would see it turn up in clinical reports worldwide.

One likely reason for a handful of households rising to power in the old past is that they simply so occurred to be surviving on fertile land, allowing them to have reliable and healthy and balanced spawns because of a wealth of food and easily accessible water.

I would not eliminate the possibility that some kind of extraterrestrial (or demonic) race is privately functioning with the Illuminati leadership and directing them in their affairs, but the subject of aliens is past the scope of this book. For the most part, the "evidence" of such beings is impossible to verify or limited to interpretations of old art or "video clip evidence" of strange flying things-- a lot of which are top secret speculative aircraft or scams. Aliens (or demons) dealing with the Illuminati is one thing-- a handful of households interbreeding with each other to maintain their "unusual ancestral tree" a secret amongst themselves is something entirely different.

CHAPTER SIX

Affiliated Secret Societies

Secret societies got into pop culture in the 21st century, thanks partly to Dan Brown's novels and Hollywood films such as The Skulls (2000) and National Treasure (2004). As the 2004 US election approached, it was well reported in the mainstream news that George W. Bush and his rival John Kerry were Skull & Bones, the now-famous secret society based at Yale University. The correct terminology is really that they "are" members, not that they "were" members, given that it is a life-time membership beginning their senior year of college.

While many people have become aware of Skull & Bones, many wrongly believe it's just an elite fraternity for rich kids, but Skull & Bones differs from a fraternity in several essential ways. First off, nobody "promises to join" the club hoping to get accepted. Instead, they recruit individuals who are seen as deserving to be members. The club does not do any charity work, which is quite familiar with a lot of fraternities, and their whole focus is tailored for members' postgraduate life, which is why somebody doesn't become an official member up until their senior year, rather than rushing a fraternity freshman year like many other college clubs.

While there are several secret societies in colleges worldwide, Skull & Bones is in a league of their own regarding their power and impact. While they are possibly one of the more well-known secret societies, there are other effective lesser-known ones.

There are secret societies of politicians, businessmen, media moguls; there is a secret society of scientists (the Jasons); there's even a secret society of secretaries, who deal with men in other secret societies. Few individuals know that there is a secret society of women designed after the Bohemian Grove, who call themselves the Belizean Grove. Much of these strange groups comprise overlapping members, and at the higher levels, work together with each other in one giant compartmentalized pyramid-shaped structure of power.

Mystery Schools

The first or initial secret societies were called the Mystery Schools, which implied that they taught the Ancient Mysteries of life and death. The word "mystic" suggests one who studied the secrets, and ancient inquisitive men formed groups or "schools" to research and consider life's most important questions. Specific expected responses were found, or misconceptions developed, intended to help man understand his presence here on this earth.

Some see the secret occult understanding originating from these Mystery Schools not as evil, but as a tool that can be utilized for either wicked or good, comparable to "the Force" in Star Wars.

Simply as guys get into relationships based upon specific interests like model airplane clubs, car meets, and many other types of clubs, men in ancient times who discovered they had a common intriguing contemplating the mysteries of life found themselves coming together in these Mystery Schools.

Numerous Mystery Schools turned up in the ancient world, claiming to, or looking for to, find the powerful secrets of life, and aim to get in harmony with the divine to receive the blessings deep space uses or describe the human condition. While these groups appear to have at one time had the sufficient intentions, many people think they were eventually destroyed and taken over by sinister men who turned the once honorable schools into a mafia of madmen who use their remarkable intellect and social media networks to shackle society. Illuminati expert Manly P. Hall discusses, "The masses, deprived of their birthright of understanding and groveling in lack of knowledge, eventually became the abject slaves of the spiritual impostors. Superstitious notion widely prevailed, and the black magicians entirely dominated national affairs, with the result that humanity still suffers from the sophistries [fallacious arguments, particularly with the intention of deceiving] of the priestcrafts of Atlantis and Egypt.".

The mystical custom, as it is in some cases referred to, appears to have begun in Mesopotamia, the oldest human civilization and the first to develop a written language. It can be traced to ancient Egypt and the Isis cults (3100 B.C.) and then over to Greece in the Eleusinian Mysteries (1500 BC), including the Demeter and Persephone cults. Throughout this time, the Dionysian Mysteries were practiced in ancient Greece and Rome and included making use of intoxicants and other trance-inducing methods to come into a higher understanding of the Mysteries.

The Dionysian mysteries were mostly based upon Dionysus, who happens to be one of the Twelve Olympians in Greek mythology, as well as the God ecstasy and wine

If you follow the chain consistently, you progress to the Pythagoreans and onto other Greek secret cults like Mithrasim (100 A.D.), then to the Gnostics (1-300 A.D.), to the Knights Templar (1118), and on to the Cathars in the 13th Century, and then to the Jesuits (founded in 1540), continuing to the Rosicrucians (1614), then to Freemasonry (1717) and continuing to the Illuminati (1776). If you keep moving ahead, when you get to more contemporary times, you'll see organizations like Skull & Bones (1832), Bohemian Grove (1872), the Federal Reserve Bank (1913), the Council on Foreign Relations (1921), the Bilderberg Group (1954), and so on.

While you may be used to some of these major Illuminati organizations, each piece of the puzzle contains numerous details. When carefully assembled, you develop a mosaic that shows a specific and typical theme. They are all hierarchical fraternities who use various routines and pageants to impart in their members that they are a select elite group of masters who know "the truth" that will enable them to become gods among men. To protect their secrets to a selected few, initiates free swear blood oaths to never reveal their understanding to outsiders or those in the lower hierarchy levels.

The Knights Templar

At this moment in time, lots of people have become aware of the Knights Templar. They might be familiar with a bit of the story surrounding them and their allegations against them by the Catholic Church. Still, a couple of individuals have taken a comprehensive look into the organization and its activities While most people think the Catholic Church made up the allegations of devil worshiping and blasphemous rituals as an excuse to seize the Templar's wealth and put them out of commission, you might be shocked to discover who confesses the accusations were real.

The Knights Templar name indicates they were the knights of Solomon's Temple, and were a group of Christian knights who offered to safeguard Jerusalem from the Muslims who were trying to capture the land. The Templars were founded in 1118 in France by a man named Hugues de Payens, who hired around nine others, mostly members of his own family, who then offered to secure pilgrims traveling from the coast of the Mediterranean to the Holy Land.

While they were committed "warrior monks" who desired to 'protect' the Holy Land, it appears the creators had an ulterior intention. While most of the growing Templar organization might have been completely committed to securing the Holy Land, the inner circle were hectic covertly excavating Solomon's Temple site for treasure and rare artifacts.

Amongst the most damning accusations made against the Templars was that their inner circle performed devilish homosexual rituals, including a Baphomet demonic idol. While most people believe these accusations were made by the Catholic Church to demonize the Templars, others have a different view. Eliphas Levi, a popular occultist in the 19th century, explains, "Did the Templars adore Baphomet? Did they provide a disgraceful salutation to the buttocks of the goat of Mendes? What was this secret and powerful association which threatened Church and State, and was hence damaged unheard? Judge nothing lightly; they are guilty of a terrific criminal activity; they have exposed to profane eyes the sanctuary of antique initiation. They have gathered once more and have shared the fruits of the tree of knowledge so that they may become masters of the world."

He continues, "Yes, in our profane conviction, the Grand Masters of the Order of the Templars worshipped the Baphomet, and triggered it to be worshipped by their starts." In the notorious Satanic Bible, published in 1966 by Anton LaVey (real name Howard Levy), Baphomet is noted as the demon the Knights Templar worshiped. So even the Church of Satan's founder accepts the allegations made against the Templars as real.

Manly P. Hall, a 33rd-degree mason, best recognized for his revealing book The Secret Teachings of All Ages, wrote, "The well-known hermaphroditic Goat of Mendes was a composite creature formulated to symbolize this astral light. It is similar to Baphomet, the mystic pantheons of those disciples of ritualistic magic, the Templars, who most likely got it from the Arabians.".

According to Hall and others, it is believed the Templars not just found physical treasure like gold and silver in their executions, but informational treasure also in the type of ancient scrolls where they discovered their unusual secret doctrine.

Researchers Knight and Lomas, who are not considered "conspiracy theorists," discussed that according to their findings, "Hence it follows that the mysteries of the craft are the secrets of faith. The Knights were, however, mindful not to entrust this important secret to anyone whose fidelity and discretion had not been completely proved. For that reason, they developed various degrees to test their prospects. They offered them just symbolical secrets without any explanation, to avoid betrayal and exclusively to allow them to make themselves well know to each other. For this reason, it was resolved to use different indications, words, and tokens in each degree, by which they would be protected against the Saracens, cowans, or trespassers."

In The History of Magic (released in 1860), Eliphas Levi reveals, "The Templars had two teachings; one was hidden and reserved to the leaders, being that of Johannes [Gnosticism]; the other was public, being Roman Catholic doctrine. They deceived in this way the enemies that they wanted to supplant. The Johannes of the adepts was the Kabalah of the Gnostics. Still, it degenerated quickly into a mystic pantheism brought even to idolatry of Nature and hatred of all revealed dogma ... They went as far as recognising the pantheistic importance of the grandmasters of Black Magic. The better to isolate themselves from obedience to a religion by which they were condemned before, they rendered magnificent honors to the monstrous idol Baphomet."

Lynn Picknett and Clive Prince also confirm the secret teaching accusations in their book The Templar Revelation, stating, "It is most likely that the bulk of the Knights Templar were no more than easy Christian solders they appeared to be, but the inner circle was different. The Templars' inner circle appears to have existed to further active research into esoteric and religious matters. Probably one reason for their secrecy was that they dealt with the arcane elements of the Jewish and Islamic worlds.

78

They sought, literally, the secrets of deep space anywhere they presumed they might be discovered, and in the course of their intellectual and geographical wanderings came to tolerate-- even to embrace, some unconventional beliefs."

These "unconventional beliefs" appear to have included what's called sex magic (typically spelled sex magick with a "k" at the end), which is the practice of including different sex acts into secret rituals in the belief that the sexual energy produced is changed into spiritual power, supposedly allowing participants to activate dormant supernatural capabilities. Theodore Reuss [co-founder of the Ordo TempliOrientis] exposed that sex magic was the best trick of occult fraternities, stating, "Our order possesses the secret which opens up all Masonic and Hermetic tricks, namely, the mentors of sexual magic, and this mentor describes, without exception, all the tricks of Freemasonry and all systems of faith." He also stated that sex magic was the big trick of the Knights Templar.

In his book to The Secret Teachings of All Ages, titled Lectures on Ancient Philosophy, Manly P. Hall again reveals some amazing occultic secrets few individuals have found about the Templars. He wrote, "It was not the physical power of the Templars, but the understanding which they had brought with them from the East, that the church feared. The Templars had discovered part of the terrific Arcanum; they had become smart in those secrets which had been celebrated in Mecca thousands of years before the development of Mohammed; they had read a few pages from the dread book of the Anthropos, and for this knowledge, they were destined to die.".

Eliphas Levi writes in agreement, "It was the memory of this religious and scientific absolute, of this teaching summarised in a word, of this word alternately lost and recovered, which was transmitted to the elect of all antique initiations ... it was this same memory handed on to secret associations of Rosicrucians, Illuminati and Freemasons which provided a significance to their unusual rites, to their less or more standard signs, and a validation above all to their commitment in common, as well as a hint to their power."

This "occult power" wasn't the only thing that resulted in their downfall. With the assistance of other secrets, the Templars likely learned from the unusual scrolls they acquired, ultimately prospered bankers who issued loans, not just to individuals, but to emperors and governments. The Catholic Church would not allow people to charge interest on money they lent to someone else because it was considered a sin (called usury). Still, the church looked the other way when the Templars did it, likely because they needed their protective services in the Holy Land.

Through giving money with interest, the Templars had exploited one of the most mysterious and compelling principles on the planet today. The Illuminati banking cartel utilizes the same method through its front groups like the Federal Reserve, the World Bank, and the International Monetary Fund.

The Jesuits

Moving forward to some hundred years later and we can see the Catholic Church following the same pattern of the Templars hoarding knowledge, wealth, and power, so insiders can live like kings by benefiting from the ignorant masses. Ignatius of Loyola established the Society of Jesus (aka the Jesuits) in the year 1540. Their members are likewise known as the "Pope's Marines" because of their militant support of the Catholic Church. The Jesuits were founded to battle against the Protestant Reformation to keep the Catholic Church in power by any means necessary. While supposedly being a Christian group the Jesuits' activities have been anything but it.

Some think that Illuminati founder Adam Weishaupt was discreetly working for the Jesuits. Still, his correspondences reveal he deeply disliked the Jesuits, although he did embrace their "ends justifies the means" strategies in hopes of replacing them with his comparable type of tyranny.

A document entitled The Secret Instructions of the Jesuits, was published in the 1600s, allegedly written by a general in the society, and exposed the techniques and "ends validates the means" code of the Jesuits. The Church declares the documents are a forgery created to libel the Jesuits, obviously, but when one becomes mindful of the criminal and callous activities Church experts have taken part in to gain and keep their power, it doesn't truly matter if they're a forgery or not, because the tactics of the Jesuits and the Vatican have ended up being commonly known.

The Catholic Church's crimes are legendary, from imprisoning Galileo for declaring the earth revolved around the sun, to the Spanish Inquisition, where officials tortured and killed anybody who dared disagree with them. And everybody is familiar with their institutional pedophile issue and the generations of cover-ups they have taken part in to secure the criminals.

These actions continue to give Christians a bad name with the majority of anti- Christian bigots obviously uninformed (or willfully overlooking) the many non-Catholic Christians (like Protestants, Methodists, Lutherans, Baptists, non-denominational groups, and so on) which were (and still are) horrified by the actions of the Catholic Church who, for centuries, held a monopoly on Christianity, albeit their twisted and un-Biblical brand of it.

Jesuits were basically to be blamed for the 1605 Gunpowder Plot in England, an assassination effort where the criminals, including Guy Fawkes, attempted to blow up the house of Parliament to eliminate King James and the Protestant aristocracy. Every November 5th, bonfires and fireworks are used to commemorate the plot's failure, an event that has come to be known as Guy Fawkes Night.

In Rome, Vatican City is not just a city, but a sovereign country owned and run by the Catholic Church that was created in 1929 by the Lateran treaty. It is only 110 acres and has a population under a thousand people and has over 8 billion dollars in assets. The Pope is the head, and is secured by his army, the Swiss Guard.

The Popes, Bishops, and Priests of the Catholic Church are essentially the very same as the Pharisees who Jesus criticized about 2000 years ago for their hypocrisy and pride due to their spiritual knowledge. One needs to look no further than the Inquisition or the enormous institutional cover-up of several pedophile priests to see the Catholic Church is corrupt to the core. The Catholic Church also diverts and perverts the many teachings of Jesus in several ways, such as having individuals admit their sins to a priest instead of to God himself, along with having a indulgences, which, if you don't know, implies that people used to pay cash to the church and in return a priest would forgive that person's sins and inform them they could then enter Heaven. Some indulgences were even sold for sins people would commit in the future. Such a practice was a disgraceful abuse of power and contradictory to the teachings of Jesus.

The Catholic Church generally took the releasing messages of Jesus and packaged them up and then offered them to the public, when Jesus had intended them to be available to all free of charge. This is the same thing the Jewish Pharisees did with Judaism, causing Jesus to denounce them openly. For these reasons and more that the Vatican, specifically the Pope, is taken a look at with suspicion regarding the New World Order and is thought by some to one day be the false prophet spoken about in the Bible.

According to Biblical prediction, the fake Christ (the Antichrist) will be a political figure and the world leader, who will be accompanied by the false prophet. This global spiritual leader will (wrongfully) confirm to the world that the messiah has gotten here when the Antichrist announces he is God. Given that the Catholic Church is attempting to reinstate itself as the only Christian authority on the planet, many people see the Pope as a prime prospect for this false prophet.

In 2007 Pope Benedict declared that the Catholic Church was the only place to provide redemption and held the only secret to Heaven. He didn't mean Christianity is the only course to salvation, a primary renter of the faith. He implied specifically that the Catholic Church was the only way to God, which all other Christian denominations were leading the people astray and were not "real" churches.

This is the same Pope who, when he was still a Cardinal (then named Cardinal Ratzinger), was in charge of covering the extensive pedophile priest network which has been operating within the Catholic Church for generations.

A 69-page document typed in Latin and drawn from the Vatican's Secret Archives bearing the seal of Pope John XXIII, was sent out to every Bishop in the world in 1962 and comprised of comprehensive guidelines and policies about keeping allegations or claims of sexual abuse a secret.

The title of the documents in Latin, Criminesolicitationies, translates to "Instruction on proceedings in cases of solicitation" and was generally similar to an earlier set of instructions issued in 1922. The documents were confirmed genuine by the Roman Catholic Church in England and Wales.

Bishops were instructed to handle child abuse allegations "in the most secret method" and were reminded of their commitment to "perpetual silence" for what the documents called the "secret of the Holy Office."

They further state, "The oath of keeping the secret needs to be given in these cases likewise by the accusers or those denouncing the priest and the witnesses." Anyone who talks about the "secret of the Holy Office" or admits openly that any victims have stepped forward were threatened with ex-communication.

All complaints or claims about sexual assault were saved in the Secret Archives of the Vatican. Daniel Shea, a lawyer for abused kids, stated, "It shows there was a worldwide conspiracy by the Church to hush up sexual abuse issues. It is a devious effort to hide criminal conduct and is a plan for deception and concealment."

Another attorney for abused children, Richard Scorer, stated, 'We always believed that the Catholic Church systematically concealed abuse and tried to silence victims. This document appears to show it. Threatening ex-communication to anyone who speaks up reveals the lengths the most senior figures in the Vatican were prepared to go to avoid the details getting out to the general public.".

This results in the dark road of sex magic, which is the most sinister secret of Satanism. The leader of the Jesuits is officially called the "Superior General," often nicknamed the "Black Pope," and is thought by lots of people to be the actual leader of the Catholic Church who wields his power from behind the scenes.

The Rosicrucians

The Rosicrucians are an intriguing secret society-type of group because the "group" started as a hoax that influenced people to form such a group (or factions) based on the strange teachings Rosicrucian Manifestos, the first of which was published in Germany in 1614. Two other manifestos appeared later, one the following year in 1615, and another the year after that, stated to have come from a secret brotherhood that comprised an Invisible College preparing to expose themselves to the world.

There are various theories regarding who the author or authors of these mysterious books were. Many people believe they were written by Johann Valentin Andrea, a German Lutheran theologian who was supposedly hoping they would help break the Catholic Church's stranglehold on power.

Whoever wrote the manifestos chose to launch them under the pseudonym Christian Rosencreut. Since the name translates to Rosy Cross-- a rose having been an alchemical sign of incredible perfection and paradise, as a sign for the work. The first manifesto states a story of how "Christian Rosencreut went on a journey to the Middle East to study the occult and the ancient secrets. The books consist of covert meanings and mystical understanding, which could only be exposed to a select couple of people.

In the texts, "Christian Rosencreut] blogged about a future utopia where people of different religions would all worship the same God in their style while having tolerance for all other views. The Catholic Church condemned the manifestos and anyone who supported them.

The books also anticipated a coming age of enlightenment arising from the discovery of ancient Hermetic secrets. Some think making it through Knights Templars were behind the mysterious manifestos, and some also credit Rosicrucianism for altering stonemason guilds into the philosophical Freemasonry we are familiar with today.

Rosicrucian researcher Christopher McIntosh wrote, "It has often been recommended that the Hiramic legend in Masonry may be related to the legend of Christian Rosenkreu] and his burial place ... It is not impossible.

That an impulse of a Rosicrucian nature (using the word "Rosicrucian" in its best sense) was entirely responsible for the improvement of operation into speculative Masonry." The transformation from "operative" masonry to "speculative" masonry" implies altering from a simple stonemason trade union to the philosophical and spiritual type of Freemasonry that exists today. The 18th degree of Scottish Rite Freemasonry is called the Knight of the Rose-Croix (Rose Cross), plainly revealing a connection between the two groups.

The Mormon Church, or the Church of Latter-Day Saints, includes several parallels with Rosicrucianism as they prefer to be called. First, both stem from books said to have been "discovered" or inexplicably appeared, which cleverly blend occult misconceptions and routines with Christian philosophy. Mormonism founder Joseph Smith Jr. most likely knew of the Christian Rosencreut] legend when he planned his tale of "finding" a supposed ancient text himself. Considering that Joseph Smith was a Freemason, he would have identified with the Legend of Enoch, which declares that the true name of God was carved into a golden delta (triangle) and hidden before the terrific flood so that it would be protected (and found) by a future generation.

These misconceptions of ancient "lost and discovered" magnificent texts mentioning past cultures and mystical secrets were the motivation for 'The Book of Mormon' which Joseph Smith claimed to have "discovered" written on a stack of Golden Plates in the 1820s, which naturally aren't in a museum someplace because he said an angel took them back to paradise for safekeeping! Smith was a Freemason who combined Masonic folklore with Christianity to develop Mormonism, which he declared "brought back" the lost secrets from the ancient past with his "discovery" (fabrication) of the Book of Mormon, again, which he amazingly "equated" from "Golden Plates" that are no place to be found.

The name "R. C. Christian" appeared in 1980 surrounding the creation of an enormous and mystical occult monolith in Elberton, Georgia-- a structure known as the Georgia Guidestones. The name was selected as a pseudonym by the individual who paid and created for this bizarre monument. "R.C. Christian," obviously standing for Rose Cross Christian, and the Brotherhood of the Rosy Cross, which was a popular calling card of early Rosicrucians. The Georgia Guidestones monument stands nineteen feet tall and displays ten commandments in 8 different languages as the New World Order's ten commandments. The very first of which is to maintain the human population under 500 million individuals. The monolith is stated to be the "Guidestones to an age of reason" and has several astrological markings in style, including a hole in line with the North Star.

It wasn't merely Mormonism creator Joseph Smith and the man behind the Georgia Guidestones who got motivation from the Rosicrucians, but likewise the early creators of Freemasonry and even the dad of the Illuminati, Adam Weishaupt. Lots of Rosicrucians in his time, in fact, denounced Weishaupt and the Illuminati for taking what they thought about to be a worthy principle of an informed brotherhood, and turned it into a system to exercise his own tyrannical goals.

Skull & Bones Society

Even if you're familiar with Skull & Bones and a few of the claims about them (numerous of which are real, by the way), the much deeper you look into this group, the more apparent it ends up being that they are anything but a common college fraternity. Since it has already been discussed earlier in this book, I won't repeat many of what has currently been covered. However, I will add a couple of more pieces to the pu]] le that many people are not acquainted with so you can get a full photo of them.

Skull & Bones was the FIRST secret society at Yale and the first senior society-- meaning somebody does not end up being a member until their senior year at Yale. There were fraternities at Yale. However, Skull & Bones started a new chapter in the school's history in 1832 when they developed the first secret society, quickly to be followed by Scroll & Key and then later Wolf's Head, the leading three senior (and hidden) societies. The three clubs even hold regular "inter-council conferences" numerous times a year to coordinate their activities.

Each year fifteen new members are recruited (or "tapped," as they say) to sign up with. They are chosen during the last few weeks of the term their Junior year to prepare them to replace the outbound seniors who lead them through the fancy and hellish initiation event where they are given a new name (Long Devil, Machiavelli, Baal, Beel] but are just a few examples). During part of the initiation, they lay in a coffin and provide an in-depth history of their sexual experiences up to that point in a routine called Connubial Bliss.

Members consider the world "their realm" and call outsiders "Barbarians." When initiated, the men (and now some women) are considered "Bonesmen" or Knights of Eulogia, which is Greek for "Knights of the Blessing." They even hold an impressive Skull & Bones wedding when some of their members get married to initiate the brand-new wife into the "Bones Family." Behind every corrupt man, there's usually a woman going to look the other way. They also own a 40-acre island situated on the St. Lawrence River in Alexandria Bay, called Dear Island, used as a personal getaway for "Bonesmen" and their households.

After the summertime, when the new school year starts, and the new beginners are then elders, they meet every Thursday and Sunday night for an expensive dinner (typically steak and lobster) followed up with "sessions" that include various lectures and arguments. It is believed that they eat their food using Adolf Hitler's spoon that a "Bonesmen" in some way obtained. Skull & Bones has its collection of books in its library located in the Tomb [headquarters] to help new members find out the world's ways. There is even a "Bones Bible" and other black books kept in the clubhouse library. They operate as a 5013c organization under the Russell Trust Association (or RTA Incorporated).

Their 2012 filings with the IRS show they invested 469,000 dollars on "individual advancement" for their members.

No form of alcohol is allowed inside the Skull & Bones Tomb clubhouse; that's how serious they are. This is not a party. Taking control of the world is a significant business.

Another difference between Skull & Bones and traditional fraternities is that fraternities usually do neighborhood or community service and assist with regional fundraisers. Still, this weird group only looks out on their own. The men (and now ladies) recruited into Skull & Bones are never engineers or mathematicians because these professions hold little power compared to those in business, banking, media, politics, and law, which are the dominant careers of the members.

You are probably, familiar with the fact that the most famous member is President George W. Bush, but many people don't know that his family has a long history with the group. Aside from his father, George Herbert Walker Bush, being a member, Prescott Bush, George W's grandfather, and his uncles John Walker, Jonathan Bush, and his other uncle George Herbert Walker III. So also was his cousin Ray Walker and his great-uncle George Herbert Walker Junior.

After George W. Bush ended up being president in January 2001, he selected several of his fellow Bonesmen to numerous high-level positions within the government. For instance, he chose William H. Donaldson as chairman of the Securities and Exchange Commission; Edward McNally was offered a job in the Department of Homeland Security. Robert D. McCallum was selected to be Assistant Attorney General; Roy Austin was offered the ambassadorship to Trinidad and Tobago; Victor Ashe was given a spot on the board of directors of Fannie Mae (the Federal National Mortgage Association), America's biggest house mortgage investor, and so on.

The list of Skull & Bones members who have got to the peaks of power is long. Co-founder Alfonso Taft became the head of the Department of War, which was the Department of Defense's name up until the government altered the name in real Orwellian double-speak style. Alfonso Taft's son, William Taft, ended up being President of the United States. Pierre Jay was the first chairman of the New York Federal Reserve Bank; Winston Lord became chairman of the Council on Foreign Relations. Percy Rockefeller was on the board of Brown Brothers Harriman & Company, which had its assets seized in 1942 under the Trading with the Enemy Act after finding the firm was helping fund Adolf Hitler.

Later on, John Kerry, who ran for president against George W. Bush in the 2004 election, ended up being Secretary of State under President Obama.

The list of significant power gamers in government simply goes on and on. Raymond Price (1951) was a speechwriter for Presidents Nixon, Ford, and Bush. When he was the Vice President, Christopher Taylor Buckley was the chief speechwriter for George H. W. Bush. Austan Goolsbee became President Barack Obama's primary economic consultant, etc., and so on. It's fascinating to mention that the father of American football, Walter Camp, was a Bonesman. As you may understand, football serves as a contemporary bread and circus distraction for most Americans, transporting their energy and aggression into viewing a lot of men chasing after a ball instead of focusing on crucial social issues. This is all part of the plan because it keeps the majority of people out of the way so the elite can perform their program.

Skull & Bones members produced the American Historical Association, the American Chemical Society, the American Psychological Association, and the American Economic Association. The atomic bomb was essentially a Skull & Bones work involving William Averell Harriman, Governor of New York, Henry Stimson, Secretary of War, McGeorge Bundy, U.S. Intelligence Officer, Robert Lovett, Secretary of Defense, and

George L. Harrison, consultant to the Secretary of War and President of the New York Federal Reserve Bank.

It shouldn't be surprising that an organization whose symbols and styles revolve around death would ultimately be responsible for developing the most deadly weapon in the history of humanity. The group's obsession with death is incredibly disturbing. All the death symbolism is meant to work as a constant reminder of their own demise. Given that they do not believe in an afterlife, they are prompted to become gods on earth during their short time here.

We often think about the society "ruling the world" in terms of political leaders and organizations, but they have also dominated the faculty of Yale University. Some reports declare that four out of five professors between 1865 and 1916 were Bonesmen.

In 1873, a students paper called The Iconoclast published a short article denouncing Skull & Bones control of Yale. "Out of every class Skull and Bones takes its men ... They have got control of Yale. They carry out their business. Cash paid to the college must pass into their hands, and go through their will ... It is Yale College versus Skull and Bones!".

Aside from being accused of controlling the professors at Yale and power positions in politics and business, they are also accused of worshiping Satan and performing disturbing rituals.

The group's favorite number, 322, possibly holds a secret satanic meaning. Many individuals think the number 322 is a referral to the Book of Genesis chapter 3, verse 22, which discusses Adam and Eve eating the Forbidden Fruit from the Tree of Knowledge of Good and Evil and using this number is seen as a recommendation to the Luciferian teaching or the satanic secret.

In 2001, a press reporter called Ron Rosenbaum from the New York Observer used a night vision camera to video the initiation routine from the edge of a nearby structure that ignored the yard of the Skull & Bones clubhouse. The footage reveals it initiates kneeling and kissing a skull, and after that appearing to take a knife and slit the throat of a naked woman who was being held down by other members.

People were also heard shouting a strange mantra, "The hangman equals death, the Devil equals death, death equals death!" The hangman most likely describes Jesus holding on the cross, and the mantra appears to convey the same significance as the riddle of the four human skulls when they are asked which one is the wise man, the beggar, the king, and the fool. The response given is that it does not matter to the fact that "all is the same in death.".

Rosenbaum was not exactly sure what to make of this behavior and asked, "Is that the trick they've been concealing since the society was established in 1832, the spin-off of a German secret society: devil worship? A satisfaction of the paranoid fantasies of the fundamentalist right, who believe the Eastern establishment is a front for hellish conspiracy."

Scroll and Key Society

The Scroll & Key society is another secret society at Yale University, created in 1842, ten years after Skull & Bones, and was the second secret society composed of seniors. Just like Skull & Bones, Scroll & Key hires fifteen new students at the end of their junior year, which they see as having the possible and determination to advance the organization's objectives. Scroll & Key is considered one of the "Big Three" senior societies at Yale- - the other two being, Skull & Bones, in addition to Wolf's Head.

Fareed Zakaria, a CNN commentator on foreign affairs, was initiated as a Scroll & Key member when he attended the university in 1986. Fareed went on to attend Bilderberg conferences (in 1993 and 2009) and became a member of the Council on Foreign Relations. He didn't simply join the CFR; he was the handling editor of their Foreign Affairs publication, which dishes out their political propaganda on a platter for the members.

Fareed once argued that the Constitution is dated and must be "fixed" to get rid of the Second Amendment to "modernize the Constitution for the 21st Century."

Other significant members include Ari Shapiro, who ended up being the White House Correspondent for National Public Radio (NPR); Cornelius Vanderbilt III of the rich Vanderbilt dynasty James Stillman Rockefeller (class of 1924), who was the President and Chairman of the First National City Bank of New York; and Huntington D. Sheldon worked for the CIA as the Director of the Office of Current Intelligence.

The Scroll & Key society run under the legal entity called the Kingsley Trust Association, which creates a guard of privacy to secure them from individuals looking for information utilizing the name "Scroll & Key" and according to their 2012 IRS filings, which should be offered for public assessment, they have over 9 million dollars in assets and invested 650,000 dollars that year.

Wolfs Head

Wolf's Head is the 3rd of the "Big Three" senior secret societies at Yale and was established in 1884, partly to counter the supremacy of Skull & Bones over student affairs. They, too recruit fifteen brand-new upcoming seniors for subscription and are now part of the bigger network, including Skull & Bones and Scroll & Key.

The club's logo is a wolf's head on an inverted Egyptian hieroglyph called an ankh, often called the Egyptian Cross and stated to symboli] e "the secret of life." Wolf's Head developed its own Egyptian themed "tomb" headquarters in 1924 thanks to a contribution from one of their members, Edward Harkness, who became John D. Rockefeller's right-hand man. Harkness himself was listed by Forbes magazine as the 6th wealthiest man worldwide throughout his life.

The club convenes every Thursday and Sunday night, where the men prepare themselves for life after college, when their real work starts. Among their most widely known members was Erastus Corning, who went on to be the Mayor of Albany, New York, for more than 40 years! Another prominent member was Paul Moore Jr., who later became a bishop of the New York Episcopal Church and one of the best-known clergy. After his death, his daughter revealed that Moore was bisexual and had a history of homosexual affairs. She detailed her father's double life in her book, The Bishop's Daughter: A Memoir. While the Bush crime family has been active in Skull & Bones for generations, they are also involved with Wolf's Head. President George H. W. Bush's younger brother William Henry Trotter "Bucky" Bush was inducted in 1960.

The service name of Wolf's Head is the Phelps Association, and according to their 2013 IRS filings, which need to be revealed since they are registered as a 501c3 tax-exempt foundation, the organization holds over $6 million in assets and spent over $373,000 on their members that year alone. The members of Wolf's Head were responsible for developing the Yale Political

Union, which is the center for politically minded students at the University.

Communism

Communism is usually promoted as a political philosophy to presumably help the typical worker fight against the "overbearing" business owners. Still, it's a conspiracy controlled by the elite who have utilized Communism as a system to encourage the development of an all-powerful state that they are in control of.

As Gary Allen puts it, author of None Dare Call it Conspiracy, "Communism isn't a movement of the downtrodden masses, but it's a movement formed, controlled and utilized by power-seeking billionaires to get control of the world... first by developing socialist governments in the numerous nations and then consolidating them all through a 'Great Merger,' into an all-powerful world, socialist super-state probably under the auspices of the United Nations.".

The Communist Manifesto, composed by Karl Marx and his mostly ignored coauthorFrederichEngles, was first published in 1848, and is commonly believed to have stimulated the Communist Revolution in Russia in 1917 and infecting other countries such as North Korea in 1948, China in 1949, and a few years later, moving to Cuba in 1953-- but what most individuals neglect is that Karl Marx was just a secretary who wrote the book laying out the Communist views for a secret society called the Communist League.

The manifesto itself goes thus; "The Communist League (previously called the League of Just Men) ... which could of course, only be a secret one ... commissioned the undersigned [Karl Marx and Friedrich Engels], at the Congress held in London in November 1847, to draw up for publication a comprehensive theoretical and practical program of the Party. Such was the origin of the following Manifesto, the manuscript of which traveled to London to be printed a few weeks before the February Revolution.".

In 1953, the California Senate Investigating Committee on Education stated thus, "So-called modern-day Communism is the same hypocritical and deadly world conspiracy to destroy the civilization that was founded by the secret order of the Illuminati in Bavaria on May 1, 1776, and that raised its hoary head in our colonies here at important periods before the adoption of our Federal Constitution."

The report goes on to say, "The acknowledgment of May 1, 1776, as the starting date of this world revolution conspiracy is easy to understand when it is realized that May Day is frequently commemorated, even in recent times, by rioting and bloodshed on a world-wide scale.".

"It was not until 1847 or 1848, that the Communist conspirators, who had previously operated in secret, came out in the open with the Manifesto of the Communist Party, by Karl Marx and Friedrich Engels, boldly pronouncing against almost everything upon which civilization is based -- God, religion, the family, individual liberty, etc.-- the concluding paragraph of the manifesto explaining: 'Communists refuse to conceal their views and objectives. They honestly state that their purpose can only be accomplished by the forcible overthrow of the entire social order. Let the ruling classes tremble at the possibility of a Communist revolution. Proletarians have nothing to lose but their chains. They have a world to win.'".

"In issuing this manifesto, the Communist conspirators think the time had arrived when, with the help of oblivious victims, a worldwide take-over could be achieved; there were not enough oblivious victims then, and the anticipated coup failed."

"The Communist conspirators thereupon developed the strategy, for the future, of supplementing the long-established secret conspiracy, around since May 1, 1776, with a constant public campaign for victims amongst the oblivious of all countries. And, in an attempt to conceal from view the underlying hypocritical conspiracy existing since May 1, 1776, it was decided that, in such a public project, the manifesto of 1848 ought to be heralded as the founding date of communism, and Karl Marx incorrectly declared as its author.".

New Age guru Benjamin Crème, who is looking forward to the arrival of the Antichrist, thinking he will turn earth into an incredible paradise, confessed, "Marx was undoubtedly a member of the Hierarchy, of a certain degree. Taking a look at the effect of his work over the years-- that could just have been the work of a disciple of some degree, an initiate of some level-- very first to have the vision, and second of all to have the capability to embody that vision so that the work might spread out."

While Christians are often stated to have eliminated the most variety of people in the name of God, the truth is that Communists have been responsible for the best genocides in the world, stopping in the name of the State (their government), in countries like China and North Korea. Over 30 million were eliminated in the Chinese Communist Revolution lead by Mao Zedong, and Joseph Stalin eliminated over 3 million in Russia in the name of Communism.161 Massive numbers have also been killed in Vietnam and North Korea by Communist revolutionaries. Belief in any God besides the government is forbidden because it lowers individuals' obligation to the State. The government is God in Communist nations.

At the heart of Communism is a huge all-powerful government that controls every aspect of an individual's lives-- from the schools to their jobs to healthcare and banking, with a little group of elite bureaucrats living luxurious lives expense of the working class. Naturally, this is one of the Illuminati's main objectives, who are promoting the idea as a romantic paradise.

CHAPTER SEVEN

Symbolism and Protocol of Illuminati

It is often said that a picture is worth a thousand words. Just because pictures contain lots of information, someone could speak for hours attempting to describe every information but still couldn't convey whatever one encapsulated. Symbols reach deep into the soul and the psyche, as it purposefully and unconsciously convey meanings and stimulate emotional reactions. We live in a world loaded with symbols. A traffic sign at an intersection implies you stop; a wedding ring symbolizes a man and woman's dedication to each other. The American flag represents the values, principles, and hard work that America is built upon. The true power of symbols originates from their ability to evoke specific thoughts and feelings.

A souvenir you purchased on a trip reminds you of all the fun you had there, and just the sight of the object promotes memories and feelings about the journey. A framed image of your favorite car hanging on the wall in your office unconsciously reminds you of the flexibility you feel on the weekends driving down the road, briefly leaving your concerns or worries behind. Family images conjure up feelings of delight and fond memories simply from glancing at them for a minute as they rest on our desk or hang on our fridge.

While we can all articulate and agree on what many symbols imply, what makes them so unique is that the same sign might have completely different meanings to different people. Let us now translate some popular Illuminati symbols and uncover their occult "hidden" meanings and see why they are used and what they imply to insiders. Most of these symbols themselves aren't "wicked" in and of themselves; they've simply been adopted by people or groups who are wicked, so different symbols have taken on negative undertones. The swastika was a popular Hindu sign of health and well-being before the Nazis included it as the Nazi party's logo; therefore, now we negatively associate what was originally a positive symbol. The symbol itself is certainly not evil, but we had come to associate it with evil when in reality, it was pirated and perverted, so for many people, its meaning has been tainted from what it originally meant to communicate.

The Sun

To the ancient Mystery Schools in the past, and several contemporary magical or knowledge groups (including the Illuminati), the sun is their main sign. It is often incorporated into their logo designs and artwork. The sun represents power and light. The word Illuminati means enlightened ones, and the word enlighten contains the name light, which originates from the sun. Someone is said to be bright if they are smart and are likewise called fantastic, which, if you look that word up in the dictionary, you will discover that it suggests "shining vibrantly."

The sun increases and brings life to the world by repelling the cold and frightening darkness of the night. It is an amazing, massive, and strange power that affects all life on planet earth. We tell the time based on the sun, it affects the seasons, and it even has an immense impact on our psyche and health. The 28th degree in Freemasonry is called the Knight of the Sun, and is simply one example of how Masons admire this enormous star at the center of our solar system.

The Pyramid

The pyramid represents society's social hierarchy, symbolically illustrating a little enlightened few at the top, and the masses of oblivious "worker bees" on the bottom. A sun on top of a pyramid symbolically represents the little number of Illuminati "enlightened leaders" at the top of the social hierarchy judging over the masses of oblivious slaves below who make up the pyramid's base.

The Dictionary of Symbols discusses, "The base is square and represents the earth. The pinnacle is the starting-point and the finishing-point of all things -- the mystic 'center.' Joined with the pinnacle to the base are the pyramid's triangular-shaped faces, symbolizing fire, magnificent revelation, and the threefold principle of development. Consequently, the pyramid is viewed as a sign revealing the whole of the work of growth in its three vital elements."

The ancient Egyptian pyramids, constructed over four thousand years ago, are still among the seven wonders of the world and have been an endless secret source even to this day. While mainstream historians think the pyramids were constructed as burial places for the Pharaohs, the Illuminati believed that they were temples where the Mystery Schools taught their essential secrets.

The 33rd degree Freemason Manly P. Hall describes, "The Great Pyramid was not a lighthouse, an observatory, or a tomb, but the first temple of the Mysteries, the very first structure put up as a repository for those secret facts which are the specific foundation of all the sciences and arts ... Through the mystic passages and chambers of the Great Pyramid passed the Illumined of antiquity. They entered its websites as guys; they came forth as gods. It was the place of the 'second birth,' the womb of the Mysteries, and knowledge dwelt in it as God dwells in the hearts of guys.".

As you may be aware, a pyramid with an all-seeing eye can be found on the back of the one-dollar bill, which many people believe is generally a stamp of ownership by the Illuminati. The man who developed this Great Seal was a Freemason named Charles Thomson, validating many peoples' suspicions that a concealed hand strategically placed the sign on the currency as a secret indication of their power.

The expression Novus Ordo Seclorum (Latin for New Order for the Ages) has appeared on the bottom of the pyramid on the dollar's back since the year 1935. At the opening of the 110th Congress on January 4th 2007, Speaker of the House Nancy Pelosi made a puzzling referral to the Great Seal, announcing, "Our Founders visualized a new America driven by optimism, opportunity, and courage. So confident were they in the new America they were advancing, that they place on the Great Seal of the United States, 'Novus ordo seclorum'-- a new order for the ages ... This vision has sustained us for more than 200 years. It accounts for what is best in our great nation: chance, liberty, and justice. Now we must bring forth that vision of a new America.".

The All-Seeing Eye

The symbol of one eye, usually with rays of light emanating from it, represents God's omniscient power and dates back to ancient Egypt, where it represented the sun God Horus who could see all. In some cases, it's called the Eye of Providence, and as you are aware, it sits on top of the pyramid on the back of the one-dollar note. This all-seeing eye sign also represents Big Brother and the Orwellian power of the intelligence companies seeing what everyone does, what they purchase, and cataloging their online activities.

Not only are there all-seeing eyes watching people in the shopping center and walking down the streets of significant cities, but the majority of people have voluntarily installed an all-seeing eye in their living-room-- and even their bedrooms-- With the click of a couple of keys, these eyes can be activated by crafty hackers or government institutions. I'm speaking about webcams that are built into televisions, tablets, and laptop computers, not to mention, possibly a lot more disturbing listening to people too through the microphones that accompany them.

While much of this has become fairly popular by now, one interesting point, a couple of individuals contemplate is that the all-seeing eye, aside from representing the Illuminati-- may end up being a sign of the Antichrist himself. One Bible prophecy about the Antichrist is that an attempt will be made on his life to secure or damage one of his eyes. Since the symbol often represents a "God," it's possible that the coming fake Christ might embody this sign as a technique to encourage the masses that he is God. In Islam, Muslims have a similar prediction saying that the Antichrist, who they call the Dajjal, will be symbolized by one eye.

Serpents and Snakes

The serpent's sign is maybe best understood as the animal in the Garden of Eden who lured Adam and Eve into disobeying God by eating from the Tree of Knowledge of Good and Evil. The word snake has negative connotations, implying someone is a liar or deceptive. While the usual sense of a snake is negative, and the Biblical story of Adam and Eve illustrates Satan as the opponent of God and humanity, the occult analysis is quite different. Occultists and Satanists praise the snake and think it brought wisdom to Mankind, allowing human beings to become gods.

Again we seek the revelations of 33rd degree Freemason Manly P. Hall who explains, "The serpent is real to the concept of wisdom, for it tempts men to the knowledge of himself. Therefore the understanding of self resulted from man's disobedience to the Demiurges, Jehovah [God]" Hall continues; "The serpent is the symbol and prototype of the Universal hero, who redeems the worlds by giving development the understanding of itself and the realization of good and evil."

The Secret Doctrine states, "The Serpent of Eternity and all Knowledge that Manasic spirit [the logical faculty of the mind], that made him find out the secret of creation on the Kriyasaktic, and of procreation on the earthly planes-- led him as naturally to find his way to immortality, notwithstanding the jealously of the Gods."

The evil scumbag Aleister Crowley had this to state: "This serpent, Satan, is not the enemy of Man, [because it is he] who made Gods of our race, knowing Good and Evil." 264.

Like Satanists and occultists, Freemasons adore the serpent as a hero and worship its wisdom. Here is a quote from Albert Pike's Morals and Dogma about the snake, reading, "It is the body of the Holy Spirit, the Universal Agent, the Serpent devouring its tail."

Complicating the meaning of the snake symbol are several cryptic declarations in the Bible, the first of which is when Jesus advised people to be as smart as snakes but as mild as doves in Mathew 10:16. This declaration appears to acknowledge that serpents consist of knowledge or represent a power that might be used for either good or evil. Another hard and intriguing to reconcile story about serpents is when Moses made a bold (brass) snake and attached it to the top of his personnel to recover the Israelites who had been bitten by snakes in the desert. The American Medical Association's logo design is a snake coiled around a person, and the same symbol is often found on ambulances as a symbol of health and healing. When somebody reaches the 25th degree of Freemasonry, they are called a Knight of the Brazen Serpent.

One of the reasons snakes have to symbolize knowledge and enlightenment is since their eyes are always open, given that they don't have eyelids. Snakes are unique animals because they have no legs but walk around, shooting across the ground like a bolt of lightning. To early Man, they might have seemed magical since they can appear out of no place and then disappear into the turf or into the earth itself. The shedding of their skin has symbolized a renewal or immortality, perhaps since primitive man believed that snakes were never-ceasing and would bring to life a new self, when a snake "dies" it would rise once again, leaving behind its old "carcass" in the form of its shed skin and continue to live on.

It's possible that the serpent does not necessarily represent evil in and of itself, but might represent a force that might be used for either good or evil.

The Phoenix.

A phoenix is a large mythical bird that symbolizes cyclical renewal, immortality, or resurrection. The animal is portrayed similar to an eagle and is usually linked to the sun. Several myths speak about the phoenix passing away, breaking down, and then rising once again out of its ashes. Some think that many of the eagle symbols we see today are covertly symbols of a phoenix, including the double-headed "eagle" that is a symbol of Freemasonry's 33rd degree.

The eagle that has come to be a popular sign of America, and discovered on the back of the dollar, is also thought to represent a phoenix occultly. The Secret Teachings of All Ages mentions that "The hand of the secrets managed in the facility of the new government for the signature of the mysteries might still be seen on the Great Seal of the United States of America. A cautious analysis of the seal reveals a mass of occult and Masonic symbols chief among them, the so-called American Eagle ... only the student of symbolism can see through the deception and realize that the American eagle on the Great Seal is but a conventionalized phoenix."

The book, released in 1928, also mentions that, "Not only were many of the founders of the United States government Masons, but they received aid from an august and secret body existing in Europe which helped them to develop this country for a specific and peculiar purpose known only to the initiated few. The Great Seal is the signature of this exalted body-- hidden and for the many part unidentified-- and the unfinished pyramid upon its reverse side is a teeterboard setting forth symbolically the task to the achievement of which the United States Government was dedicated from the day of its in conception."

The phoenix has been suggested to be the name of the new unified international currency that global banksters have long-awaited. The cover of the January 1988 edition of The Economist magazine reads "Are you ready for a world currency" and had a short article that explained, "Thirty years from now, Americans, Japanese, Europeans, and individuals in lots of other rich nations, and some fairly poor ones will probably be paying for their shopping with the same currency. Prices will be quoted not in dollars, yen, or D-marks but in, let's say, the phoenix. Because it will be more practical than today's national currencies, the phoenix will be preferred by shoppers and business."

The metaphor of "rising from the ashes like a phoenix" describes a rebirth or something being eliminated or destroyed to bring to life something new, and so by eliminating the U.S. Dollar and other currencies around the world through inflation, the banksters are symbolically bringing to life their new currency, which many are planning to call the "phoenix."

The Owl

When discussing Illuminati significance, the owl is most known for its connections to the Bohemian Grove, the Illuminati's summertime retreat in northern California. Esoterically, the owl represents wisdom because it sees in the dark, and Adam Weishaupt picked the Owl of Athena as one of the Bavarian Illuminati symbols. Early civilizations saw the owl as mystical because it is just seen at night, considering that they are nocturnal animals.

The Dictionary of Symbols describes, "In the Egyptian system of hieroglyphs, the owl symbolizes death, night, cold and passivity. It also relates to the world of the dead sun, that is, it is of the sun which has set below the horizon and which is crossing the lake or sea of darkness."

A tiny owl can also be found hidden on the one-dollar bill, perched on the upper left corner of the frame surrounding the "1" located in the upper right-hand corner of the bill. Many individuals see an owl made into the street design of Washington D.C., right on top of the U.S. Capitol building when viewing the area from overheard or taking a look at it on a map.

Images of owls are often seen in classrooms based on a small stack of books to symbolize knowledge. The National Press Club's logo design also consists of an owl standing on a book. Owls are also viewed as guardians, and typically owl statues are put on the top of structures to frighten other birds.

The Skull and Crossbones.

The skull and crossbones symbol has a sinister appearance, which is why dubious groups have been utilized for centuries-- from pirates and bicycle rider gangs to the Nazis. It represents death, or the power over life and death, which is why it interest megalomaniacs and psychopaths. The Nazi officers in charge of concentration camps where over six million people were eradicated wore a skull and crossbones sign on their uniforms, the same emblem utilized by the Skull & Bones secret society as their logo. The Nazis called it the Totenkopf (German for skull or dead man's head), and it was a blatant declaration of their objective. Hitler personally handed out a Death's Head ring to elite SS soldiers.

Since they were dedicated to battle or fight to the death and promised never to be taken alive as a detainee, the Knights Templar incorporated the symbol into their lives. Some Freemasons have a human skull sitting on their desk to remind them of their death and the fact that their life is ticking away quickly. It is meant to prompt them to work towards achieving their objectives before it's too late.

As earlier discussed, both the Bavarian Illuminati and Skull & Bones society at Yale use the object in their induction ceremony with their four different skulls. The question about which one is the fool, the wise guy, the beggar, or the king. The answer to this induction riddle, "Whether rich or poor, all's the same in death," is implied to enhance their mortality to them and remind them that the clock of life is ticking, so they had better do all they can to end up being kings here in this life because when you're dead- - to them-- absolutely nothing matters. The riddle is indicated to convey that they do not believe in an afterlife or a last judgment from God.

Baphomet

Baphomet is an occult idol that is illustrated as an androgynous man with female breasts with the head of a goat. Prometheus's torch is often protruding of its head and linking serpents is rising from its crotch. It's a strange and ugly looking figure that dates back to the 1300s when the inner circle of Knights Templar integrated it into their rituals and secret doctrine,

An early depiction of the figure comes from an 1854 book entitled Transcendental Magic written by a French occultist Eliphas. Giving support to his illustration, Eliphas Levi stated, "According to some, the Baphomet was a monstrous head, but according to others, a demon in the kind of a goat. A sculptured coffer was dug up recently in the ruins of an old Commandery of the Temple, and antiquaries impressed upon it a Baphometic figure, corresponding by its credit to the goat of Mendes and the androgyne of Khunrath."

Several Satanists have proudly integrated the Baphomet figure into their signs and routines. Aleister Crowley wrote that the snake or the "devil's emblem" was Baphomet, who he also called the "hieroglyph of arcane perfection."

One variation of the figure is the Church of Satan's logo, printed on the cover of The Satanic Bible. While many people claim that the Catholic Church made the claims that the Knights Templar were utilizing it in secret routines as an excuse to detain them and seize their wealth throughout the Inquisition, most Satanists and occults hold the belief that the Catholic Church's claims were true.

Again, Eliphas Levi boldly declared in his book Transcendental Magic, "Yes, in our profane conviction, the Grand Masters of the Order of the Templars worshipped the Baphomet, and caused it to be worshipped by their initiates."

The Pentagram

An upside-down pentagram drawn within a circle is among the most apparent and familiar symbols utilized by occult organizations, defiant teens, and rock stars today. It is a lower level occult symbol typically utilized to represent dark powers or sinister forces. Because it's so extensively understood, it's never truly utilized by high-level occultists or the Illuminati, who instead use much less familiar symbols like all-seeing eyes, pyramids, black and white checkerboards, owls, and other less polarising images.

A pentagram differs from a regular five-pointed star in a couple of methods. A pentagram is drawn using five straight lines to make up the points and form a pentagon in the middle. The Satanic pentagram is drawn upside down and often incorporated by a circle. Satanists use it because Christians originally utilized the five points of a pentagram (called the pentalpha) to symbolize the five wounds of Jesus (the two spikes through his hands, two through his feet, and the spear that pierced his side). Satanists like to pervert things and turn Christian signs upside down or backward to signify their opposing views and beliefs, and this is how their use of upside-down pentagrams came into existence.

The Dictionary of Symbols entry on the star reads, "As far back as in the days of Egyptian hieroglyphics a star pointing upwards represented 'increasing upwards towards the point of origin' and formed part of such words as 'to raise,' 'to educate,' and 'the teacher.' The inverted five-pointed star is a sign of the infernal and utilized in black magic."

In Freemasonry, the pentagram is called the Blazing Star and represents the sun, Lucifer, carnal understanding, and power. To Wiccans and Pagans, the star's five points represent air, fire, water, earth, and spirit. The female branch of Freemasonry, called Eastern Star, uses an upside-down pentagram as their emblem.

Square and Compass.

A square (the tool utilized by carpenters to layout an ideal angle or a "square" angle) overlaid on top of a compass (the tool used for drawing arches and circles-- not the navigation tool for recognizing directions) is a popular sign in Freemasonry and is frequently seen with the letter G in the middle. The square and compass symbolize the alchemical teaching of "as above, so below" or the joining of earth and heaven by forming two opposite facing pyramids with one pointing up and the other pointing downward. The letter G in the center means God or Gnosis (the Greek word for knowledge). It is also usually stated to represent the "Great Architect of deep space," a term many masons utilize to describe God.

The Statue of Liberty.

If you asked the typical American what the Statue of Liberty represented, they'd most likely inform you it involves "America," "liberty," or "democracy." Some may understand that it was provided to America by the French. Still, few know its very design and development was managed by Freemasons, the secret society, not France's government, who then gave it to America as a "present" and placed it in New York Harbor.

Frederic Bartholdi, the designer of the Statue of Liberty, was, of course, a Freemason, and knowledgeable about occult and Illuminati importance and philosophies. The three significant figures included with the Statue-- Frederic Bartholdi, who developed the statue itself; Gustave Eiffel, who created the inner assistance structure; and Richard Hunt, who created the pedestal-- were all Freemasons.

Bartholdi's original plan for a huge statue of this type was put in a harbor in Egypt. After the Egyptian government rejected his proposal, he changed his style slightly and approached America to see if he could erect his recently created statue in the United States. The point is, he initially wanted to construct a bizarre "God-like" figure and have it stand somewhere other than America. Bartholdi's first choice for his mystical statue was Egypt, not the United States.

The initial name of the statue was "Liberty Enlightening the World," not the "Statue of Liberty." Once again, the word Enlightening fits in with the Illuminati style-- Enlightening, knowledge, light, the sun, intelligence, bright, brilliance, Lucifer.

A near mirror image of the Statue of Liberty stands in France, also on an island, in the Seine River in Paris, set up in 1889, just three years after the one in America was completed. If it's an "American" symbol, why is there an almost similar one in France? There are, in fact, numerous almost identical "Statue of Liberty" figures all around the world, including Leicester, England; Lviv, Ukraine; Carinthia, Austria; Cenicero, Spain; Arraba in Israel, and lots of other places.

The Statue of Liberty is a modern-day variation of the Colossus of Rhodes, a 100-foot-tall statue portraying the Greek sun god, Helios (Helios being Greek for sun) in ancient Greece. The Colossus was created in the third century B.C. and depicted Helios (the Sun God) holding a torch high in one hand and stood on the island of Rhodes dealing with the water. "This massive gilded figure, with its crown of solar rays and its upraised torch, signified occultly the wonderful Sun Man of the Mysteries, the Universal Savior," states The Secret Teachings of All Ages.

A poem is printed on a plaque that sits prominently near the base of the Statue of Liberty entitled The New Colossus, plainly signaling that it was imitating the Greek sun god. A Masonic cornerstone ceremony was carried out when construction began.

A Masonic plaque was positioned on the site—the statue is a composite of a range of ancient goddesses who represent the womanly concept.

The torch that the Statue of Liberty is holding represents Prometheus's torch, who occultly symbolizes Lucifer. The Greek mythological story of Prometheus is the same allegory of taking fire (i.e., knowledge) from God or the Gods, and giving it to people, therefore outraging God.

Here is Manly P. Hall again, one of Freemasonry's greatest thinkers, explaining in Lectures on Ancient Philosophy, that, "Man wandered hopelessly in the gloom of mortality, dying and living without light or understanding in his thrall to the Demiurgus [the developer God] and his host of spirits. At last, the spirit of disobedience entered the creation in Lucifer's form, who, in the guise of a snake, tempted man to revolt against the demands of Jehovah (the Demiurgus). In Greece, this character was called Prometheus, who brought from the gods the impregnating flame that would launch the life latent in this wide range of germlike potentialities."

The seven horn-looking spikes coming out of the Statue of Liberty's head represent rays of the sun, and symbolically represents the spirit radiating from the mind as enlightenment or "knowledge." There are seven of them because the rays represent the seven liberal arts and sciences, therefore consisting of a necessary knowledge base. The statue is also holding a book, symbolic of information and knowledge-- once again fitting in with the style of enlightenment and knowledge, because knowledge is power, which the Illuminati has.

Rockefeller Center's Prometheus.

In New York City, Rockefeller Center is a substantial 22-acre complex made up of nineteen different buildings and the home of Bank of America, NBC, General Electric, and other major international Illuminati-controlled corporations. Standing plainly within the property is a big gold-colored statue of Prometheus holding a ball of fire in one hand as he flies through the air. The mythological Greek story of Prometheus stealing fire from the Gods and offering it to humanity regardless of the punishment he will deal with is seen by occultists as identical to Lucifer's story providing humanity the knowledge of good and evil that God had forbid us to have.

This statue that stands outside of Rockefeller Center is a homage to Lucifer, which goes undetected by the average individual not acquainted with Illuminati symbolism. Many people are most likely not even know about the Prometheus myth, or have long forgotten it since studying Greek mythology in high school and just believe the statue is just another random piece of art with little or no significance.

Helena Blavatsky describes in her traditional occult work, The Secret Doctrine, that, "The allegory of Prometheus, who takes the magnificent fire as to enable men to proceed consciously on the path of spiritual advancement, hence transforming the best of animals on Earth into a prospective god, and making him free to take the kingdom of heaven by violence. Hence, Zeus's curse is pronounced against Prometheus, and by Jehovah [God] against his 'defiant son,' Satan."

So as you can see, it's not just me making the connection between Prometheus and Lucifer-- It's occultist experts themselves. It's no coincidence this stands on a Rockefeller home, a family with generational ties to the Illuminati establishment.

The Washington Monument

The Washington Monument, which lies straight west of the United States Capitol structure in Washington DC, standing around 555 feet high, controls the sky throughout the city and can be seen from miles everywhere, particularly at night with the traffic signal shining from the top appearing like the evil Eye of Sauron in the Lord of the Rings motion pictures. The monolith is an Egyptian obelisk with a pyramid capstone on the top and was completed in 1884.

The structure is among the most important symbols in America to the Illuminati, although most people are uninformed of its covert meaning. Occultists see the monument as a massive phallic symbol-- a big penis-- representing manly energy and supremacy. One would anticipate the "Washington" Monument to be a statue of George Washington himself, similar to the Lincoln Memorial's substantial figure of Abraham Lincoln Rather it's a giant erect penis of the Egyptian god Baal. Naturally, it was developed and built by Freemasons, who ever had a ceremony to lay the foundation when building started.

FritzSpringmeier, author of Bloodlines of the Illuminati explained, "Every early morning when the United States President awakens, he can watch out the window, see the Masonic obelisk and be reminded of who controls America. I the president has any training in the Mystery Religion of Egypt he will also understand what body part is symbolically set up in the Washington Memorial."

Springmeier goes further to state, "If the U.S. were ever to go back to serving God, that monument would be a great one to destroy. God asked the Israelites not just merely to avoid worshiping such abominations. He asked His people to ruin them, for their very creation was an abomination."

Cleopatra's Needle.

While the Washington Monument might be the most well-known Egyptian obelisk in America, it isn't the only one. Another one stands in Central Park in New York City-- called Cleopatra's Needle, and this one is an authentic Egyptian obelisk that dates back to around 1500 B.C. and is transported to New York in 1881.

Comparable "Cleopatra's Needles" actually stand in London and Paris, symbolizing the Illuminati's guideline in those nations as well. Not surprising, there is also one in Vatican City. The one in New York's Central Park stands 70-feet tall and weighs 220 tons. Why and how it was brought to America from Egypt is an intriguing story.

For some reason, Henry G. Stebbins, the Commissioner of the Department of Public Parks in New York in the 1880s, revealed he was looking for assistance financing a strategy to bring the statue to America. William H. Vanderbilt, who was one of the wealthiest guys worldwide, was asked to help make it occur and contributed over $100,000 (over $2 million in 2014 dollars) to assist. Remarkably, the shipping expenses for the one sent out to London were spent for by Dr. Erasmus Wilson, a Freemason.

When the obelisk arrived in America, thousands of Freemasons took part in a parade as it was rolled up Fifth Avenue from 14th Street to 82nd Street. The Grand Master of Masons in New York performed a foundation-laying ritual as a celebration when it was put up at its last destination in the park. When it initially got here in New York in 1881, Cleopatra's Needle was covered with plainly noticeable hieroglyphics about the sun god Horus, but most of the carvings have since been alert far from acid rain. While they endured 3000 years in Egypt, it seems the ancient relic was no match for the contamination of New York City.

Music and Movies

For hundreds of years, knowledge of the Illuminati and their symbols was mostly contained within the Mystery Schools that taught the esoteric custom. Outsiders didn't even hesitate about most occult signs because they were viewed as common art, and a couple of individuals paid much attention to them. With the birth of the information age, things started to change. In the 1990s and early 2000s, a growing variety of online forums and sites were dedicated to examining secret societies and exposing these little known issues to a wider variety of individuals.

For years, those interested in such things were thought about a fringe minority of patriots and "conspiracy theorists." Still, with the emergence of social networks becoming a standard feature in many people's lives, and with video sharing websites like YouTube altering the nature of media and information exchange, a fascinating phenomenon started to occur early in the twenty-first century. Illuminati and occult significance overflowed from what was mainly the topic of fringe websites, and "computer system geeks" on Internet forums, to end up being part of popular culture, finding its way into various traditional video and blockbuster motion pictures.

While a sizable portion of the population has become acquainted with using Illuminati symbols in rap videos and supposed "Illuminati hand indications" being flashed by celebrities, many people who notice this element of the symbolism hardly have a fundamental understanding of the history of the signs or their significances. Many individuals who have heard the frequently farfetched claims about "Illuminati stars" have dismissed the presence of the Illuminati all together as a conspiracy theory or think it's merely a secret society in Hollywood that leading celebs are part of.

While there certainly have been countless allegations made against a variety of celebrities like Jay-Z, Lady Gaga, Beyoncé, Kanye West, and several others, when you take a good analysis of stars as a whole and the power their music and personas have over the culture, it becomes obvious that music is not always "just entertainment.".

As the Illuminati prepare to announce the "royal secret," as they call it, by declaring that Satan is the King of the Earth and the "hero of humanity," hoping to finally topple the "inferior" and "evil" Creator God to finish the New World Order "utopia," celebrities have just recently played a major part in paving the path to the apocalypse.

132

The large majority of the public praise celebrities who operate as contemporary Gods that form our cultural attitudes and beliefs because their every action is imitated. Every opinion they voice is viewed as profound.

The public is growing to see the Illuminati-- not as a hazard to their freedoms or a corrupt mafia of bankers, political leaders, and entrepreneurs--. Still, as a "cool" group of great men, they wish they might be a part of it. The ethical or moral decay and disintegration of the work ethic have resulted in the typical person being happy to do almost anything for just a taste of the Illuminati's "success." Popular culture has begun representing the Illuminati as holding the secret to success or a secret society of the abundant and famous.

Occasionally movies have portrayed the Illuminati or an affiliated group as the villain in a plot to communicate a warning to the audience. Some celebs have publicly knocked them as the shadowy puppet masters pulling strings in worldwide affairs, but the overwhelming bulk of mainstream media content and celeb idols paint the Illuminati as holding the master key to success. As an outcome, many individuals would almost kill their mother to join them to have a bigger piece of the pie.

CHAPTER EIGHT

"Ex-Illuminati Members"

Similar to government whistleblowers or career criminals developed into informants who reveal the closely concealed of their organization, a handful of people have stepped forward throughout the years declaring to have been included with the Illuminati in one way or another, and offer up what they declare to be insider information about the activities and goals of the network. Most of these individuals are total scams and are merely con artists attempting to sell books and lectures or simply delight in the conspiracy community's attention, considering that numerous people believe their stories, sinker, hook, and line.

There is a detailed analysis of John Todd and William Schnoebelen, who are 2 of the most popular men who have made such claims; however, there are likewise others whose stories have spread out everywhere on the Internet like urban legends, so in this book, we'll determine and take a close appearance whether there is an authenticity to them.

Far none of the declared "defectors" have used up any evidence to back up their claims; however, they have just told tales based on the openly understood info about the Illuminati's history, beliefs, and activities. None of the "former members" has ever revealed any brand-new info that wasn't currently published in literature widely available in the conspiracy culture. However review some of the of the YouTube videos featuring their claims You will see that a too sizable percentage of the audience ultimately believes these individuals and see them as brave whistleblowers who "left" their dark past and are now on a mission to "expose" the Illuminati.

An astute student is committed to reality and doesn't approach these people's stories with confirmation predisposition. If one has diligently done their research of the errors and fabrications stick out like aching thumbs. For those who are new to examining the Illuminati, or to Tuite gullible, these "former Illuminati members" just serve to confirm their greatest fears The majority of these "defectors" are just gifted writers providing publicly known details from a first-person perspective as if they witnessed it or took part in it.

Some of these people are psychologically ill and may believe what they are stating, but the evidence proves one after the other to be phony.

Let's take a close appearance at some of these individuals stories so we can avoid them and future hoaxers from tricking people who are searching for responses and precise details concerning the Illuminati and the New World Order.

Doc Martius

Joseph "Doc" MarTuis (born upon October 26th 1956) is allegedly a previous U.S. Army medic, which is how he says he got his label "Doc," and is one of numerous self-proclaimed "previous Illuminati members" who says he was born into an Illuminati household now is dedicated to "exposing" them.

" Doc," who claims to have been raised as a seventh-generation witch, says when he was three-years-old, his household brought him to an occasion and committed him to Lucifer in a satanic baptism. For the next ten years, he says, he remained in the "external court" of the Illuminati, which he referred to as a hellish seminary school where he found out about the approaches and secret signs, and what he declares are the "eight nights of human sacrifice" that Illuminati members allegedly commemorate.

According to his story, when he was thirteen-years-old, he was "a new member of the Illuminati" after signing his name in his blood in a book made from lambskin, which he called the Book of the Dead, which so happens to be the name of an ancient Egyptian scroll containing information on how to navigate through the afterlife to participate in Heaven.

Four years later, when he was seventeen, "Doc" says he underwent another initiation ceremony and became what he called a Master Witch, or a High Druid Priest, which granted him "automated authority over a region of the United States" where he supervised over 1000 other Illuminati members. This all happened before he even finished high school! He says his superiors then bought him to join the United States Army to assist the Illuminati infiltrate the militaries. Within two weeks of being stationed at Fort Lewis in Washington, he states he had twenty individuals recruited for the Illuminati. A couple of months later on says he had more than a hundred more! In reality, the real Illuminati more likely includes nothing more significant than a couple of hundred men; however, when "Doc" MarTuis was simply seventeen-years-old, he states he was "in charge" of over 1000 of them!

Throughout an online lecture produced by Prophecy Club, he says he practiced human sacrifices eight times a year and had "continuous interaction with Demons." Marcus claims to have personally seen dozens of human sacrifices before he "went out." Still, no police have ever shown any interest in him and have never considered him to be a suspect or a witness to any murders whatsoever. On the other hand, Garbage television provided him a platform to spread his rubbish in the late 1980s. He was as soon as a guest on The Oprah Winfrey Show, where he was discussing all these expected murders and stated, "The thing is, we didn't get body bag these individuals later on. We'd simply take them [and], throw them in the woods, on the side of the roadway on a highway. Somebody's going to find them." Of course, nobody ever has because these "victims" do not exist.

The "8 nights of human sacrifice" that MarTuis claims to have commemorated was cooked up from the eight celebrations that Pagans celebrate (or Sabbats as Wiccans call them), which are commemorated throughout the year on solstices, equinoxes, and the four mid-points in between, none of which involve human sacrifices. I'm not stating that Satanists don't dedicate human sacrifices still to this day, because such events have been well recorded, but the closest MarTuis has come to one was enjoying a scary motion picture.

Regional authorities would have taken him into custody to question if there was even a shred of evidence to support his claims and no one involved with such crimes would attempt to speak about them out of fear of being apprehended. Indeed, in the 1980s, before the Internet, an average person might not easily verify or negate most claims made about the Illuminati and the occult. Very few people understood much about the topic at all. This led to the "hellish panic" in the 1980s when stories like MarTuis' were spread through tabloids and garbage TV talk shows, triggering individuals who didn't know any better to believe Satanists were abusing children and sacrificing individuals in neighborhoods throughout the country.

" Doc" states that in between dedicating his evil deeds, he was repeatedly asked by Christians if he wished to go to church or if he knew Jesus. For whatever reason, despite being a "high-level Illuminati master," he decided to go to church on Easter Sunday in 1979, where he realized he was "offered out as a slave of Satan," ended up being a Christian, and "left the Illuminati."

In among his video lectures entitled Arrival of the Antichrist, he can be seen giving the typical history lesson about Adam Weishaupt and the formation of the Bavarian Illuminati, their structure and goals, and reveals the all-seeing eye on the back of the dollar while informing the audience to take out their wallets to look at the dollar themselves as if this was some major revelation. The eye on the back of the one-dollar expense has become so primary and Illuminati 101 that most middle school trainees are now familiar with it, but back in the 1980s and 90s, when MarTuis started providing his lectures, things were Tuite various.

After his discussion on the dollar symbology, he goes on to cover the famous quotes from Pike's book, Morals and Dogma, and then shows the fascinating designs in the street layout of Washington D.C. and then grumbles about the federal government, the dumbing down of America, the Constitution, the demonization of Christians, and so on, etc. He concludes that the Illuminati will state martial law and is establishing a New World Order for the antichrist's reception.

When performing my research study into the Illuminati and encountering Doc MarTuis' claims of being a former Illuminati member, I carefully listened to his lectures online, which, like almost every other self- proclaimed "previous Illuminati member," didn't expose a single shred of info that wasn't currently extensively understood. Not only that, however, a number of his claims are ludicrous to anybody who has standard knowledge about the Illuminati conspiracy.

For instance, he states that they place a $10,000 bounty on anyone's head who tries to leave. After he "left the Illuminati," he says they attempted to kill him six times! The Illuminati can assassinate world leaders and other presidents, but they've stopped working over twenty times to eliminate this man? Absurd.

Of course, there are no authorities reports or news stories about any of these alleged murder efforts against him. Because the Illuminati is the most effective secret society globally, they would have no problem killing anyone, mainly no-name losers like "Doc" Martius.

He sells a DVD called Frontmen of the Illuminati, which includes nothing more than a badly produced home video of him sitting at a table showing different pictures of signs and people while discussing the Illuminati. The information on a website selling his DVDs checks out, "Doc MarTuis is a former Satanist who was trained in the Illuminati Plan before he came out of the coven to become a Christian. In 1992, Doc was worked with by the Boston Police Department to train their homicide detectives on how to find evidence in a criminal offense scene that the criminal was a practicing occultist. Doc likewise has appeared or the following TELEVISION programs: Oprah Winfrey, Geraldo Rivera, Hard Copy, and Inside Edition. He is the author of numerous books, videotapes, and audio cassette series and has appeared as a skilled witness in several documentaries.".

His claim of having worked with the Boston Police department has not been validated, and to believe that this guy would be hired to "train" murder detectives is absurd, particularly after having declared to have killed a lot of individuals in hellish rituals! I think the police simply decided to forgive him for all those supposed murders!

Marcus has also claimed to have degrees in sociology and history, and once claimed he would quickly be getting his doctorate in psychiatry from Baptist Christian University in Shreveport, Louisiana. Still, it was later on revealed he wasn't even participating in the school. He then said the school would be accepting a book he was composing on the occult as his doctoral argumentation!

Martius wrote several books (as does every supposed "Illuminati defector") to make a couple of bucks off the conspiracy community. Martius and other "Christians" who claim to be "previous Illuminati" members like Bill Schnoebelen and John Todd, while being total phonies might, in their mind, really believe that they are assisting people in finding out about the

Illuminati conspiracy. After all, there is a massive conspiracy, and these people do expose a few of them. Still, their produced pasts and long lists of lies about being personally included with the Illuminati when they don't even have some of their standard truths directly reveal that men like Doc MarTuis are not just scams, however quite shameful and useless too.

Leo Zagami

Another man claiming to be an Illuminati defector who went on to give interviews and lectures about the wicked plans he learned while supposedly "inside" the secret society is Leo Zagami (born in Rome on March 5th, 1970). While other alleged defectors declare to have ended up being born again Christians after "leaving the Illuminati" and state that Jesus assisted them reali] e they were on the wrong path and discovered support from Christian audiences, Leo Zagami instead has taken the New Age angle. He firmly insists the Illuminati hold "the reality" but are a corrupt group of enlightened ones who have pirated the Mystery School teachings, so he decided to leave the Illuminati to preach their philosophy to the masses.

To assist spread the "enlightening truth" kept suppressed by the Illuminati, Leo Zagami claims to have started a brand-new "faith" called Matrixism based on the popular Matrix movies! He says he began this new "faith" in 2004 to celebrate the 100th anniversary of the "deliverance" of Aleister Crowley's Book of the Law, the brief bloodthirsty book Crowley claimed was dictated to him by a devil while he was going to Egypt in 1904. Yes, Zagami is a fan of dirtbag Aleister Crowley, whose philosophies he thinks about "the truth."

His website described his brand-new "faith" as, actually having been inspired by the Matrix movement pictures, however, insists it was "conceived by a confidential group in the summer of 2004 and has brought in over 16,000 followers."

The explanation goes on to state, "The Matrix trilogy, together with associated mass media equipment such as computer game, is usually considered to be the 'spiritual text' of the movement." He says The Matrix films and computer games are "sacred texts" of his "religion." He also says the "faith" can be traced back to a book called The Promulgation of Universal Peace, published in 1922 that includes a series of speeches provided by Abdu' l-Baha, the creator of the Bahá' í Faith. All of these details, he states, comes from his knowledge of being an "Illuminati Grand Master" himself.

Zagami's site declares that he is "a high-ranking Illuminati Grand Master, who got considerable attention in the conspiracy research neighborhood between 2006 and 2008 as a defector and whistle-blower." He went by the name Khaled Saifullah Khan after having allegedly converted to Islam, but later changed his name back to Leo. He claims that his goal is to organize now "the Knights Templars of the Apocalypse" to combat the Illuminati, and says this "group" has hired 12,000 soldiers from the U.S. Military, CIA, FBI, etc., who are going to stop the "Dark Illuminati plans."

In Leo's mind, the primary enemies of humanity are: The Jesuits, which he calls "the head of the snake"; Zionists, who he states are "the financial arms of the Vatican New World Order"; the United Nations, which is "a corrupt organization in the hands of the Jesuits and their Zionist allies devoted to enslave mankind"; and "all spiritual fundamentalist because organized religious beliefs in all types and shapes is a legal mafia manipulated by the Vatican and Jerusalem in the hands of corrupt individuals who work for the elite families and their intelligence services to keep our race in ignorance and superstition in the end of times.".

Despite Leo's rambling and weird history and his new "faith" that he produced based on The Matrix movies, and his claim to still be involved with the "good" Illuminati and the "Knights Templars of the Apocalypse" and other undercover "Illuminati Resistance" members in the CIA, FBI, military, and authorities; and regardless of revealing no new details about the operations of the Illuminati-- some completely gullible fools think that he really was, or still is included with the secret society.

Leo Zigami's claims never acquired anywhere near the traction of other supposed "defectors" before him, such as John Todd or

Bill Schnoebelen, because he's not a gifted writer like some other hoaxers. And we were into the info age by the time Leo decided to step on the scene (in 2006), whereas John Todd began his talks in the 1970s, and Bill Schnoebelen in the early 1990s before the Internet was entirely used by many people who can now quickly check claims online. Even with this resource at people's fingertips, nevertheless, a stunning variety of people still think the stories from "ex-members" like "Doc" MarTuis, Leo Zagami, John Todd, and others.

Many individuals delight in conspiracy home entertainment or conspiratainment as I call it, and have little or no issue about real facts or the truth. They simply love the cleverly cooked up tales by individuals who are influenced by real events or conspiracies. After that, they manufacture an often amusing conspiracy folklore based upon grains of truth. It's sort of like a great sci-fi story that's based in part on real technology and then extrapolates into a dream created to captivate the audience.

Supreme Rockefeller.

A man calling himself "Supreme Rockefeller" and claiming to be a member of the popular Rockefeller family developed a little a stir on the Internet in 2010 after announcing that the Rockefellers were launching a strategy to fund the structure of the Third Temple in Jerusalem in what was called the "Temple

Now Project." The Third Temple describes the restoring (again) of Solomon's Temple in Israel, which was initially destroyed in 586 BC by the Babylonians, and later restored to be also destroyed by the Romans in 70 AD. Christians believe that when the temple is reconstructed for the third time, it will signify the satisfaction of one of the final predictions worrying about the increase of the Antichrist and the return of Jesus.

Presently, a Muslim mosque called the Dome of the Rock stands on the ruins of the temple, and the only way Solomon's Temple can be restored on that area is if Israel inhabits and ruins the mosque that part of the land. This is why the "Rockefeller" announcement of supposed strategies to construct the Third Temple captured many individuals' attention.

A couple of official websites released a press release about the 'Supreme Rockefeller" plan without verifying his identity or the supposed plan's authenticity. With websites like CNNMoney. Com and MarketWatch having the press launched posted, that was all the evidence numerous conspiracy blogs needed to keep up the story that a person of the last Biblical prophecies will be fulfilled thanks to the Rockefellers.

None of this was real, nevertheless, and "Supreme Rockefeller" didn't exist. The scam guy was determined as a high school dropout called Kris from Louisiana, born in 1975. While living with his mother, he worked as a cashier at a quick food dining establishment and attempted to earn money by betting and selling ringtones on different websites.

After he was fired from his job for apparently stealing, the thirty-four-year-old then began passing "Supriem Rockefeller" online and saying he was the secret kid of David Rockefeller Jr. "Supreme" posted online about how he was authorized to finalize the New World Order and "exposed" that the Rockefeller household had come down from the Annunaki, the supposed ancient race of aliens, who are thought by some to be accountable for the production of humans.

It appears his "Temple Now Project" hoax was an effort to receive donations from individuals who wished to support the plan, wanting to meet Bible prediction. One news release claimed he would be "raising funds to go towards developing the Third Temple in Jerusalem in stringent coordinance with The Temple Institute, Rabbi Hiam Richman and The Palestinian National Interest Committee (PNIC)," and his mission was to "build the Temple and to produce a One Israel-Palestine state.".

What made this hoax credible for some, aside from the Christian prophecy of the Third Temple, was the straightforward Jewish plan to accomplish this same task one day. Ever since 1987, a non-profit Jewish group called the Temple Institute has been working to do just this. In 2008 they revealed they had the High Priest's garments currently made along with do] ens of other products they intend on utilizing in "sacred routines" once it is rebuilt. Naturally, the Temple Institute had nothing to do with "Supreium Rockefeller," however, he skillfully included their name in his press release to include an aura of trustworthiness to his claims, given that they are an open group working to accomplish this objective.

This hoax didn't last too long, and his Facebook page was soon deleted. Still, many Jews and Christians continue to await the actual rebuilding of the Temple, an event that will be seen by Christians as one of the Bible's final prophecies being satisfied because, in this Temple, it is thought the Antichrist will announce himself to be "God" and order individuals of earth to praise him as such.

In the 1970s, 80s, and 90s, Illuminati phonies managed their frauds with a remarkable amount of success. While the Internet can put an end to the majority of these frauds rather quickly today, countless people are simply lost in the sea of info readily available on the internet and continue to spread out Illuminati scams far and wide, thinking every word. These are the same kinds of people who believe that whenever a famous celeb dies from a drug overdose, vehicle mishap, or health issue-- they believe they were actually "killed" by the Illuminati or fabricated their death. If you browse YouTube for keywords like "Paul Walker Illuminati Sacrifice," "Michael Jackson Murdered by Illuminati," or "Tupac eliminated by Illuminati," you will find hundreds of videos with millions of views literally and countless comments from people who are 100% convinced the Illuminati lags every celeb death.

The "Supreme Rockefeller" Third Temple hoax is not the very first time that somebody has impersonated a member of the well-known Rockefeller household. A man who called himself Clark Rockefeller (genuine name Christian Karl Gerhartsreiter) was sentenced to 27 years in jail for murdering his proprietor's kid, which put an immediate end to his elaborate scam.

Gerhartsreiter even asked his spouse into believing he was a Rockefeller for several years by taking extreme steps to hide his genuine identity. To accomplish this, he had his better half file her earnings taxes as a specific instead of jointly as many married couples do, so his real name would not need to be on the couple's income tax return, which she more than likely would have noticed. He even created their marriage license to avoid having her see his real name.

Another guy calling himself Christian Rockefeller (genuine name Christopher Rocancourt) scammed tens of countless dollars from rich people in New York in the 1990s through phony investment rip-offs after they believed he might increase their wealth because they thought he was a Rockefeller.

Saly

The list of people who have stepped forward claiming to be previous members of the Illuminati are primarily men, however in 2006, a female calling herself "Svali" turned up on the Internet declaring to come from an Illuminati family in Germany who then transferred to America when she was too young. "Svali" stated when she was a kid; she was informed that she was "special," which the Illuminati had big plans for her. At 12-years-old she underwent her "initiation" at the Vatican, as she declared all the Illuminati management's management do. By the time she was twenty-two, she was the youngest person in the "Illuminati leadership council" in Southern California.

" Svali" stated that secret Illuminati meetings were held three times a week in Escondido, California, which is a lower-income location inland where no wealthy or influential members of the Illuminati would ever go, let alone select to live. I have lived near this area for over 15 years and have buddies who have lived in Escondido, and I've seen the city with my own eyes many times. It's mostly a Mexican ghetto and would be the last place in the world the Illuminati would ever think of going.

The security for these "Illuminati" conferences, she said, was a "spy" who had actually climbed into a tree with a walkie talkie to find unwanted visitors and would then radio ahead to the group so they could "leave within five minutes." I guess the group would just run off into the woods if the individual in the tree saw anybody unforeseen rolling up to your home! You'd believe the Illuminati's security information would be a bit more sophisticated than somebody climbing up into a tree with a walkie talkie! Her claims get dumber by the second the more she informs her story.

The source of information coming from Svali appears to lead back to Greg Szymanski, who wrote (or might continue to write) for a little known site called ArcticBacon. Com, among many amateur websites, includes posts about the Illuminati, the Jesuits, and other conspiracy problems. "Svali" supposedly connected and contacted him with her claims, so he then interviewed her in January of 2006 on his practically new Internet radio show. Audio of the interview can be discovered if you can require yourself to listen to more than 30 seconds of her incoherent rambling, YouTube.

In the interview, she stated her adult co-conspirators would "get up in the middle of the night to attend conferences," and while the adults were doing their thing, the kids were "finding out how to march and shoot guns and were being trained in martial arts." She declares her initiation at the Vatican included child sacrifice. Throughout the interview, she was extraordinarily forgetful and had a tough time describing her story, which isn't even remotely convincing. However, Greg, the interviewer, ate it up and appeared to think every word she was stating, as did a measurable variety of individuals on the Internet who took place to come across her story.

When she was socializing with the Illuminati, she claimed to be a "head programmer" associated with mind control programs but never provided any details about her supposed duties and could not even articulate the fundamental ideas or history of mind control.

Svali isn't even a creative hoaxer like some others before her, and appears to be a psychologically deranged person just looking for somebody to pay attention to her. It's likewise possible that Greg Szymanski, the man who initially interviewed her, crafted the Svali hoax himself by dealing with a female friend to concoct the whole story so he could be the person to have the "unique" interview and permanently be linked to her as the person who initially "broke her story."

His site is just among countless virtually unidentified sites in the sea of conspiracy theories online, so it makes no sense why a "former Illuminati member" would connect to him since there is a great deal of relatively well-known conspiracy sites that cover such topics. She did attempt to have an e-book entitled " Breaking the Chain: Breaking Free of Cult Programming; however, it's not even listed in any of the significant e-book shops and appears like an unsuccessful attempt to attempt to make a couple of bucks by offering a PDF file from a site.

I can confirm to the reality that I have received several e-mails from different individuals making exceptionally bizarre claims such as being stalked or pestered by cults, and the incoherent and rambling nature of their emails reveal that they are from psychologically disturbed and crazy people sounding much like this female.

Actual Illuminati members are educated, smart, and well spoken individuals. They are persuading and very convincing none of which can be attributed to Svali, whose stories are so convoluted they're hard to follow as she jumps from faith to belief. How did she eventually "get away" the clutches of the Illuminati? Well, she said she left the organization because she started to realize, "what I was doing was wrong." Now that she is a "former member," she is a born once again Christian and has repented of the activities she claims to have taken part in. Today, the lady says she's a "diabetic educator" living in Texas with her hubby and two children.

The bio on the site of the man responsible for performing the interview checks out, "Greg is primary and first a satirist, an author and a reporter," so he was most likely merely trying and playing a function to have a good time with conspiracy theories by producing a new Internet urban myth of conspiracy theory fiction about the "lady who left the Illuminati."

Brice Taylor

A female calling herself Brice Taylor (a pseudonym) published a book in 1999 entitled Thanks For The Memories: The Truth Has Set Me Free! The Memoirs of Bob Hope's and Henry Kissinger's Mind-Controlled Slave, where she details what she states is her account of being a CIA mind control victim who was utilized as a sex servant Illuminati.

David Icke, a famous conspiracy author, best known for his theories that the Illuminati are an alien race of shape-shifting reptilians, is listed as a recommendation on Amazon. Com's listing of the book, in addition to Ted Gunderson, a previous FBI Agent from Los Angeles who stated, the book "verifies truths provided by lots of other witnesses."

With recommendations by such massive players in the conspiracy world as David Icke and Ted Gunderson, many individuals are inclined to believe her claims; however, upon even a quick analysis of the book, the female's story Quickly goes from being hard to think to be impossible and ridiculous by any stretch of the creativity.

This story's first wobbly leg comes when we discover Brice Taylor is simply a pseudonym and the authors' real name is Susan Lynne Eckhart Ford, who admits that she suffered from numerous character conditions from a young age. "But as I started to recover and remember more of my hidden past, I realized that routine abuse was simply the mind control injury base my ritually mistreated, set pedophile father, Calvin Charles Eckhart, and others used to condition me for involvement in the still-active supersecret Project Monarch, the Central Intelligence Agency's white slavery operation that belongs to MKULTRA and its various sub-projects," she writes.

"The outcome of several years of trauma, deliberately caused on me by my father and others to produce within me split personalities, was that I was transformed into a programmed, totally robotically slave that might not remember to tell or think what took place to me, due to the mind control and sophisticated programming I was under. I was frequently used in child and teen prostitution and pornography. By my pre-teen years, I had many characters particularly configured to be the best sex servant with government mind files and a photographic memory equipped to deliver (most often through sexual encounters) messages, some puzzling, to leading federal government authorities, performers, and other world figures."

She writes that when her memories began returning to her at the age of thirty-five she, "began having vivid, in-depth memories of being used both as a sex servant and human mind file computer system to some of our nation's highest level federal government officials in and out of the White House." She then lists Presidents John F. Kennedy, Lyndon Johnson, Gerald Ford, Ronald Reagan, George Bush, Jimmy Carter, Henry Kissinger,

155

Nelson Rockefeller, Bob Hope (the popular entertainer), and lots of others as men she says all abused her.

When she was four months old, Taylor states that while meditating, she began to keep in mind things all the method back to! (Not four years of age, four months old.) She states her dad worked as a welder who owned a welding shop in Los Angeles; however was also secretly working for the CIA as a mind control developer. "My father started the strenuous training and deliberate abuse needed to shatter my base character to produce lots of different private personalities for training and usage by others as I aged."

Her mother too, she says, was under mind control and "was listening to music she was told to listen to keep her memory of our life locked deep within her subconscious mind, while the programmed reality of herself and our 'perfect delighted household' was kept alive through configured expressions in the music."

Most of the book consists of rambling and prolonged tales of supposed abuse by such a long list of individuals, both popular and regular individuals in her neighborhood, that reads like a parody of a poorly written horror story. Individuals included in the conspiracy include her ballet instructor, her medical professional, her dental professional, her choir teacher, her next-door neighbor, individuals at her local church (who she says all had tunnels under their homes connecting them and likewise resulting in the church); the owners of the local bowling street were also in on it, and naturally the Freemason Shriners, and even the owners of a regional gas station! They were all sacrificing kids and shooting snuff films or involved with the "CIA's mind control program," she states.

The list of her alleged abusers and human-sacrificing CIA Satanists she was included with simply goes on and on. Prince Philip, Prince Charles, and even Sylvester Stallone are on her seemingly endless list of abusers. She declares that Sylvester Stallone directed several bestiality films where she says she made love with dolphins and other sea creatures! Other stars such as Jane Fonda and Barbara Streisand were likewise under mind control, she states, and Elton John was aware of such things and attempted to help the victims with the lyrics in his music.

Aside from noting half the people in her neighborhood as being "in on it," and a dozen celebrities and presidents, she likewise names some odd places where she states everyone sexually abused her or "programmed" her with mind control. Among these expected places as Disneyland, where she says her father presented her to Walt Disney himself when she was five years old, she made her appearance into a View-Master box, including dead individuals and dead felines.

" Brice Taylor" stated she would also fulfill Henry Kissinger at Disneyland, where he would "program" her using CIA mind control techniques. One of these "shows sessions," she stated, required to be carried out in front of a carrousel for some unknown factor. "I also continued to be taken to Disneyland for base shows for my new global mind file system," she composed. Who would have believed the CIA was using Disneyland as a secret mind control? Like I stated, her book reads like a bad parody of a horror story written by a teen.

She goes on to claim she was likewise asked to about McDonald's around the nation and "programmed there too." And naturally, she says she was also taken inside the National Archives, the State Department, NASA, the Pentagon, the Federal Reserve, the World Health Organization, and other military bases around the country, and insists she was "set" at each. Her handlers would require to take her to the Federal Reserve Bank to "program" her using mind control techniques. These claims are outrageous and the outcome of another over-active imagination of a crazy person or by a horrible writer fabricating such tales wanting to sell many books to the conspiracy neighborhood.

She wrote that she was even told that she would be killed in a couple of years and her services would not be needed any longer. Why would her handlers notify her that they would kill her at some point in the future? Wouldn't they keep this to themselves and lead her on? After all, if she understood she would be killed soon, would not this offer her even more reason to betray them and leave before this occurred? The more of Brice Taylor's story you read, the more unreasonable it gets, well beyond the point of rubbish.

The question remains ... why would this lady comprise all these dreadful things that she says taken place to her? What would force a female to compose such a book? I speculate that the only truthful part of the book is that perhaps she was sexually abused as a kid, but not by any of the political figures or celebs she pointed out, but at the hands of a relative or maybe even her dad. She might feel justified and achieve some healing degree by venting her anger and betrayal in a fictionali] ed book. She has projected that the perpetrators of her abuse are guys in high positions of power within society. It's likewise likely that she wrote the book only as "conspiracy fiction," wanting to pass it of as accurate to the frequently gullible conspiracy neighborhood.

Some individuals believe her claims are because there are grains of fact (albeit small little grains) considering that the CIA did do horrific mind control experiments in their MK Ultra program They did drug, hypnoti] e, and torture people in those experiments attempting to develop mind-controlled servants. In 1994 the United States federal government awarded 7 individuals $100,000 each in monetary payment to explore them,374. Still, Brice Taylor (whose real name is potentially Sue Ford) never even went to court over her claims and was not one of the receivers.

A couple of years before Brice Taylor's book was published, another lady named Cathy O'Brien released a book entitled The Transformation of America, where she had claimed to be a test subject for the CIA's MK Ultra program and a "sex slave" of the Illuminati's top political leaders. O'Brien even claims to have been taken inside Bohemian Grove. It's most likely Brice Taylor was influenced by Cathy O'Brien's book and hoped she could make money by making similar claims. While Brice Taylor is a fraud, Cathy O'Brien's claims are a bit more believable (however perhaps fabricated) and analyzed.

"Jess LaVey"

A guy calling himself "Jess LaVey" stating he was the boy of Anton LaVey, the infamous founder of the Church of Satan and the author of The Satanic Bible, threw his hat into the conspiracy home entertainment ring around the year 2000 and got himself a small quantity of attention on a couple of Internet radio shows who eagerly took the bait and offered him a platform to spread his rubbish.

" Jess LaVey" not only claimed to have been the kid of Anton LaVey (whose real name was Howard Levey by the method), however also said he climbed up the ranks of Satanism all the way approximately the Illuminati. In one interview "Jess" claims, "I never could forget the counsel of thirteen, they were very wicked looking guys. When I reached the age of twelve, my father told me I needed to go before them. They cautioned me of what could happen to me if I did not do as they suggested. George H.W. Bush Senior was among these men. I stood before them and told them I was not going to follow their ways, and I was not going to take my papa's location, and that there was nothing they could do to me. I told them I think in a higher power which greater power said in His Word that no damage could concern me.

After he refused this "invitation" to the Illuminati, he says they castrated him as his penalty. He also talked about the Kimball-Cherokee Castle in Sedalia, Colorado, a 1450s design castle developed in the 1950s on a 3,100-acre cattle ranch in Colorado. He claimed the Illuminati fulfill every year to make human sacrifices. "Satanists come together and do offensive things. To think that Bush and his entire household belongs to this example is tough for some people to believe. The entire Bush family is Satanists. He is a cool guy for Satan. Like a lethal weapon. Other "expert" hellish "leaders" have stepped forward throughout the years, generally in the 1980s and 90s such as Mike Warnke and Stephen Dollins, attempting to use their expected "satanic credentials" to enhance their new career as Christian evangelists; however, most were never included in any organized cults or groups and wildly exaggerated the expected activities they declared to have gotten involved in.

In 2002 John W. Morehead of the Watchman Fellowship, a group that monitors the activities of cults, was given a copy of what "Jess LaVey" claimed to be his social security card, which was fake and when the number was run for a background check it was shown to be void.

" Sadly, lots of have declared to be LaVey's child to acquire financial backing from churches and to provide credibility to their ministries supposedly resolving Satanism and the occult," Morehead informed Charisma Magazine in 2002.

Anton LeVay, Aleister Crowley, Helena Blavatsky, Manly P. Hall, and other real occult insiders have revealed a lot of information to see exactly what is going on in numerous Satanic groups and secret societies; however, conspiracy bilker appear to keep developing the idea that they can make some cash by claiming to have been an "insider" who is offering a "first-hand account" of what they have supposedly seen and done.

The interviews "Jess LaVey" can be discovered on YouTube. After listening to one for about 5 seconds, any sane adult ought to be able to tell he is making up his story practically as he goes along and does not even have the faintest tip of authenticity. Anton LaVey (again whose genuine name was Howard Levey) had two children and only one son; a boy called Satan Xerxes, born in 1993.

George Green.

An expected previous investment banker named George Green declares to have once attended secret Illuminati conferences where men were making "god-like choices as to who lives and who dies" and pondered "dropping neutron bombs" on major American cities to reduce the population following the Georgia Guidestones.

In his interview, which can be seen on YouTube, Green speaks about the World War Three looming in the Middle East, a coming one-world currency, FEMA concentration camps, the coming economic collapse of America, the prepared extermination of the majority of the world's population to save the earth's natural deposits for the elite, and rattles off a list of popular plans of the Illuminati. Green doesn't reveal an ounce of brand-new details whatsoever. Like numerous others, it discusses the same old widely available claims while presenting them from an expected expert who says he sat in on the meetings. He, too, is attempting to offer a book entitled Chaos in America, which never gained much traction.

If George Green did participate in any of the Illuminati meetings, he would have the ability to expose some formerly unidentified details about their plans; however, instead, he simply recycles the same old material that has been drifting around the Internet and patriot circles for lots of years. A fascinating phenomenon in the info age is that if you claim to have some sort of Illuminati "scoop" and toss the video online, individuals are going to find it, and individuals will believe it.

Aside from the common Illuminati talking points about the Georgia Guidestones, FEMA camps, and the collapse of America, George Green goes directly into crazy town and states the Illuminati have been making " synthetic individuals." He's not speaking about secret cloning programs, which most likely exist; he claims that most presidents have been "replaced" by these synthetic clones! That's right. He states our significant world leaders are all grown in an Illuminati lab and are simply pretending to be real individuals.

To "prove" this is occurring, he points to the movie Boys from Brazil, a 1978 movie about Nazi researchers producing Hitler's clones to reconstruct the Third Reich. This cloning technology, he states, was provided to us by the "greys" (aliens). He says he knows this.due to the fact that while operating in the Air Force, he claimed to have "supersecret" clearance, which offered him access to some dead Nordic-type aliens called the Pleiadians who concerned earth from the Pleiades star cluster.

While aliens may be directing the Illuminati, and leading secret human cloning programs more than likely do exist, George Green's discussion is so poorly carried out and unconvincing, it reeks of a scam from the very moment he opens his mouth. And again, he hasn't supplied a single piece of new "proof" that wasn't already widely understood by most conspiracy researchers.

Not to discuss, no one has been able to validate any part of his expected background as an "investment lender" or having any kind of "super-secret" security clearance in the armed force. Once again, we're living in a world where numerous individuals think Tupac faked his death, which simply shows that some people will think practically anything, no matter how crazy it is, despite zero evidence, and defying all reasoning and good sense.

CHAPTER NINE

The Structure of Power

Now in the U.S, the Middle East region was to be organized along the lines established by late British imperialism, which World War I acknowledged that direct colonial rule was no longer feasible. Regional management, therefore, would be entrusted to an "Arab.

Exterior" of weak and pliable rulers, with "absorption" of the colonies "veiled by constitutional fictions as a protectorate, a sphere of impact, a buffer State, and so on," a gadget more economical than direct rule (Lord Curzon and the Eastern Committee, 1917-18). We must never run the risk of "losing control," John Foster Dulles warned. The Facade would consist of family dictatorships that do what they are informed and guarantee profits to the United States, its British customer, and their energy corporations. They are to be secured by regional enforcers, preferably non-Arab (Turkey, Israel, Iran under the shah, Pakistan). British and U.S. muscle stand in reserve, with military bases from the Azores through North Africa to the Indian Ocean and the Pacific. The system has operated with sensible effectiveness over a substantial duration, and has new potential customers today.

Successes have been dramatic. Inexpensive oil fueled the "golden age" of postwar development. "Profits beyond the imagine avarice" enriched Western corporations,13 also assists in keeping the ailing British economy afloat, later on, the U.S. economy as well. The postwar settlement perpetuated the separation of the big population concentrations of the region from the oil wealth, retained in the hands of the Facade with sparse populations to share it. Apart from its unfairness, this "insanely manipulated ownership of home worldwide's most greatly armed region, with a long history of volatility and violence, is a continuous recipe for destabilization and violent upheavals," Dilip Hiro warns. "An increasing variety of Arab intellectuals and spiritual leaders," he composes, are coming to share the perspective articulated by Saddam Hussein on August 10, 1990; nevertheless, they may dislike the author of the sentiment. In Saddam's words: Through its partitioning of the [Arab] lands, western imperialism founded weak mini-states and set up the households who rendered it services that facilitated its [exploitative] objective. Hence it avoided most of the kids of the individuals and the [Arab] country from benefiting from their wealth. As a result of the brand-new wealth entering the hands of the minority of the [Arab] country to be made use of for the advantage of the immigrant and the few new rulers, social and financial corruption spread in these mini-states and from there to numerous quarters of the bulk of the Arab nations.

The United States opposes democracy in the region, Hiro writes, since "it is much simpler to manipulate a few ruling families to secure fat orders for arms and guarantee that oil price remains low than a wide range of policies and personalities bound to be thrown up by a democratic system," with chosen governments that may show popular require "self-reliance and Islamic fellowship." Hence the determination of Washington's policy of "supporting dictatorships to maintain stability" (Ahmad Chalabi), and the admitted preference for the "iron fist."

Hiro's analysis is persuasive. The roots of policy lie deep in firmly established institutional structures of power, with results that have long been evident worldwide. The fundamental policy thrust is periodically acknowledged with some regret by world leaders. Reflecting on British policy in the Middle East, Prime Minister Harold Macmillan found it "rather sad that circumstances oblige us to support reactionary and truly rather outmoded routines because we understand that the brand-new forces, even if they start with moderate opinions, constantly appear to wander into violent revolutionary and highly anti-Western positions." We require only add the usual gloss: a "violent advanced position" might be nothing more than one that seeks an independent course, becoming " strongly anti-Western" when that course is disallowed by Western power, a disaster that has been enacted over and over once again.

Rights accrue to regional actors by their position within the three-tiered tactical conception. At the regional level, the Facade of supervisors has rights, as long as they do their task; otherwise, they will be squashed. For internal "stability," the "iron fist" has often been preferred, precisely as the State Department presently discusses through the medium of the Times chief diplomatic correspondent. The local guardians likewise have rights, as does the British assistant. And the United States naturally has rights without credentials. Kurds, Palestinians, slum-dwellers in Cairo, and others who contribute absolutely nothing to the standard structure of power have no rights, by the most primary concepts of statecraft. Perhaps they can periodically be used in one or another power play, but that is where their rights end. Much of the modern history of the Kurds show these realities, as when they were supported in their revolt versus Iraq in the early 1970s in the interests of Washington's Iranian client, then delegated be butchered when that episode was effectively terminated, leading Henry Kissinger to comment acidly, in action to criticism, that diplomacy is not to be confused with missionary work. Current events, evaluated previously, include another awful chapter to the story.

Today, it is not hard to comprehend Eisenhower's lament that "the problem is that we have a project of hatred versus us, not by the federal governments; however, by the people." One may ask, however, why that should have currently held in July 1958, when the words were spoken, not long after the United States had expelled Britain, France, and Israel from the Egyptian area they had actually conquered in their 1956 intrusion, and well before the "special relationship" with Israel was in location. It is easy to discuss the hatred in Iran five years after the repair of the shah. Washington's rejection of attempts to carry out independent advancement was also unlikely to have elicited warm sensations. A year of CIA operations in Syria might shed further light on the matter.

Syria had typically been pro-American, but private U.S. intervention "assisted reverse a century of relationship," Douglas Little observes in a review of these operations. In 1948, the CIA approached Chief of Staff HusniZaim to discuss the "possibility of an army supported dictatorship," a result attained when Zaim toppled the government a few months later. Zaim authorized the Aramco oil pipeline (TOPLINE) concession according to U.S. wishes, and required peace talks with Israel, providing to transplant 250,000 Palestinian refugees, a diplomatic opening that Israel chose not to pursue. Zaim was toppled a few months later on. In 1951, Col. AdibShishakli toppled the federal government and set up a military dictatorship, with private U.S. assistance. Matters drifted out of control again. In March 1956, Eisenhower authorized Project OMEGA, which intended to overthrow the progressively pro-

Nasser program in Syria as part of a more basic strategy weaken Nasser. Operation Straggle, arranged jointly with British intelligence to topple the government of Syria, was timed (obviously, at British initiative) for the day of Egypt's invasion which France and Britain had concealed from Washington Perhaps Britain's objective was to keep the United States preoccupied elsewhere. In any occasion, Syrian counterintelligence had uncovered the plot, and it quickly deciphered. Several further clandestine operations looked to subvert Syria's government, leading lastly to a bungled CIA effort again permeated by Syrian intelligence.

The "Eisenhower Doctrine," authorized by Congress in March 1957, licensed the president to supply help, including U.S. troops, "to secure and secure the territorial stability and political independence of such Middle Easter nations, requesting such aid, against overt armed aggressiveness from any country controlled by global communism." While Egypt was the publicly designated offender, U.S. authorities thought that Syria was more "almost under the control of international communism, Douglas Little concludes. Completion result of years of such machinations was hostility to the United States, close Syrian relations with the USSR, and much hysteria in Washington about "losing the whole Middle East to Communism."

The resemblance to Cold War history in Latin America, Southeast Asia, and Africa is apparent, and its sources in U.S. policy are easy enough to discover.

CHAPTER TEN

From Demons To World   Rulers

There are levels of demonic forces that are attacking the world. These vary from demonic attacks on individuals, to principalities that look for dominion over countries or regions, to "world rulers" that look for dominion over the entire earth.

When the terrorist leader Osama bin Laden prophesied that America would fear from north to south and east to west, he issued a demonic prediction that was a clear indicator of the opponent's strategy against America. Since the opponent is always looking to counter God's work, we can understand for sure that it is God's preparation for faith to be launched in America from north to south, east to west. We are, in truth, close to another Great Awakening sweeping over America.

As the opponent steps up his assault across the world to dominate diplomacy with worry and terror, we can be ensured that it is the biggest chance for faith to be launched in every position the opponent attacks. Faith is much more powerful than worry, and faith will ultimately prevail.

The governments need to combat the war against terror on natural weapons; however, only the Church can attain the ultimate victory over this opponent. As we are told in Ephesians 6:12, "For our struggle is not versus flesh and blood, however versus the rulers, against the powers, versus the world forces of this darkness, against the spiritual forces of wickedness in the heavenly locations." This is not a war against flesh and blood; it is a spiritual battle that must be fought with spiritual weapons if we will have a true and lasting triumph.

Satanic forces assault individuals in the very same way that a principality attacks a city or area. They both start merely by looking to gain influence. They increase their influence up until they have control over the actions of those they are seeking to dominate. When this happens to a private, it is called being "possessed" by devils. Lesser levels of control by them are normally referred to as demonic injustice. Cities, regions, and even nations can be possessed by the more powerful forces of evil.

Christians are provided authority over satanic forces. No Christian who has come to understand our Lord Jesus Christ's authority must worry about being had by satanic forces. It releases God's authority to cause satanic forces to fear us and run away from us if a Christian is strolling in faith. Recognizing, facing, and erupting devils is regular, scriptural Christianity.

The next level of wicked authorities resolved in Scripture is called "principalities and powers." As specified, these are more effective than devils, and they look for rule over regions or countries, not simply individuals. Every Christian has the authority to cast out satanic forces; we do not cast out principalities and powers; rather, we must "wrestle" with them to displace them. This level of warfare is addressed in other books I have written, such as Epic Battles of the Last Days, Mobilizing the Army of God, and A Prophetic Vision for the 21st Century.

There is another, greater realm of evil called "world rulers." These do not simply affect individuals or areas; however, they can control much of the earth. This level of wicked I attend to in my book Shadows of Things to Come. Above this level is the wicked lord, Satan himself. Christians have contacted us to battle evil on all these levels. We just have true spiritual authority to the degree that the King lives within us or the degree to which we abide in the Lord. As we grow in authority, which is evidenced by our increased faith, we will be called to battle battles on greater levels.

Normally, only demons will have people, and the fight that many Christians deal with is personal. This is mainly with the evil that attempts to gain entryway to our own life. As we are victorious on this level and are trusted with more spiritual authority, we may be gotten in touch with to challenge evil on a high- er level, seeking the liberation of an area or perhaps a country from the enemy's domain. As my good friend Francis Frangipane likes to say, "With brand-new levels come new devils." This might not be too motivating, but among the ways that we understand, we have been promoted in spiritual authority is by the larger satanic forces that we need to combat.

Francis has written what numerous think about to be the greatest book ever on spiritual warfare, The Three Battlegrounds. He describes how our battle against evil starts with the fight in our minds in this timeless message. As we get victory there, we should then fight for the success of the Church. When the Church is triumphant in an area, will it displace the principalities over it, only?

If we are provided national or global spiritual authority, we can depend on attacks from principalities and powers. If we have been offered authority that will impact the whole earth, we will have to face a world ruler eventually. Paul, the apostle, was such a man, which is why he needed to face Caesar. Since Jesus is the highest authority in the Kingdom, He needed to be challenged by satan himself and prevail.

Since Caesar's scope of authority, he was not being manipulated by a simple satanic force, however, by a world ruler. Satan has to use males to do his will just as the Lord works through His individuals. As one grows in spiritual authority, they will be buffeted by those managed by more powerful demonic forces. This is not something that we ought to fear, as the one in us is much greater than all of the evil one's power. To be assaulted on a higher level should be an encouragement to us.

There are watershed events that cause sweeping changes over the entire earth. You can count on a world ruler being behind them if these occasions are evil. We saw such an occasion on September 11, 2001. This was the start of another tactical assault of worry on the level of a world ruler. This did not simply impact the United States; the entire world was shaken that day. The civilized governments of the world should now make terrorism the world's primary enemy it is. This is a spiritual opponent that can not be defeated by simple bombs and bullets. Christians must get rid of the fears that control their own lives, and then the Church needs to overcome the same. Then we should rise to the place of faith and authority where we confront the world ruler that is assaulting the entire world.

The Two Mandates

To understand that the genuine war is not natural and spiritual is not to negate the righteousness of the war in which our earthly governments are now engaged. As we are informed concerning them in Romans 13:1 -4,.

Every person is to be in subjection to the governing authorities. For there is no authority except from God, and God established those which exist. For that reason, whoever withstands authority has opposed God's ordinance; and they who have opposed will get condemnation upon themselves.

For rulers are not a cause of worry for excellent habits, however, for evil. Do you want to not worry about authority? Do what is good, and you will have praise from the same; for it is a minister of God to you for good. But if you do what is wicked, hesitate, for it does not bear the sword for absolutely nothing, for it is a minister of God, an avenger who brings rage on the one who practices evil.

As this passage states, civil governments have a mandate from God to avenge evil and bring rage on those who practice evil on the earth. For this factor, civil governments have been given the sword or military power. We must always wish our governments and for their success in bringing the rage of God on those who practice evil. Throughout the Bible, we see that many of the time when the Lord satisfied His Word by bringing judgment upon a country or individuals, it was done by using the military power of other nations.

Civil government is necessary for keeping order to the degree that it is possible until the Kingdom of God pertains to restore righteousness and justice on the earth. It will never be worked out entirely because fallen men exercise this authority. It does at least restrain the forces that would bring about a complete meltdown of order and authority. God ordains civil authority; however, we should not error it for the Kingdom of God's authority.

A Different Spirit

As Christians, we have a different requirement of authority. We are not here to avenge evil in this age, but in reality, we are required to like our opponents and hope for them. Our warfare is not against people, but against whatever has people in chains. The greatest triumph of all would be the repentance and salvation of our enemies. Many Christians have a tough time understanding the two various mandates offered to federal civil governments and the Church. However, this is something crucial that we should settle in our hearts if we will be efficient in our task of taking apart the spiritual fortress that keeps males in bondage.

Our civil governments are battling a righteous war versus evil as they fight terrorism or governments that promote terrorism. However, the Church has contacted us to a much various battle. We are called to battle the hidden war that is being waged in the heavenly places. Ours is a spiritual war.

This does not suggest that Christians can not join the military forces of countries to fight the war on the level of civil authority. They need to comprehend that while marching under civil governments' orders, their authority will be worked out through their physical weapons, not their spiritual ones. This does not suggest that Christian soldiers must not hope and try to use their spiritual authority, too, however when you're in battle don't drop your gun to do so! You must not think twice to use the weapons that the federal government has given to you for battling if you are under orders from a civil government.

Also, if we are operating under the required provided to the Church, we do not have the authority to utilize the weapons utilized for battling flesh and blood for our fight. This is why "Christian militias" that arm themselves with weapons or other physical weapons will always be inspired by worry and paranoia. They are managed by the wicked since they are not correctly under either of the mandates of authority God has offered to men.

Fight the Good Fight

Spiritual authority is something that we grow into. We are offered more authority as we grow spiritually and are given higher commissions by the Lord. This will be evidenced by an increase of faith to brand-new levels. We see in the Book of Acts that Paul the apostle was called as an apostle lots of years before he was commissioned to that ministry. With that commissioning came authority on a greater level. However, "... many are called, but few of are chosen" (Mt. 22:14). One interpretation of this is that numerous are called; however, few persevere through all that is needed to receive their commission.

Being called to a high position does not immediately give one authority. Maturity and the loyalty that goes on to possess the promises will launch true authority. How - ever, we should comprehend that spiritual authority is not offered so that we get more regard from individuals, however, so we can combat effectively against the powers that are destroying people.

Our first objective should be to face and conquer our demons and our worries, so that we can grow in authority to handle larger satanic forces and set other people free. Because there is a faith that gets rid of the world, nothing less than this can be our goal to conquer the evil that is now controlling the world. We may not see wicked fully displaced up until the King Himself returns to earth, but there is a scriptural mandate for us to do all we can to prepare the method for His coming Kingdom by getting rid of evil in every manner in which we can now.

I have heard lots of reveal fear that this can be brought too far. I am rather sure that if we get brought away with excessive faith and take down some fortress of evil that we were not contacted us to tear down, saving more souls than we were contacted us to set free, I believe the Lord will forgive us!

Among the ways the enemy has kept much of Evangelical.

Pentecostal and Charismatic Christianity in chains has been to impart a belief that since it is unavoidable, the entire world will be up to the antichrist, it is ineffective to eliminate the evil worldwide, and therefore we must just attempt to be devoted ourselves and wait on the Rapture. Some Scriptures challenge his deceptiveness, such as the one we priced estimate in an earlier chapter, Daniel 11:31 -32.

We understand from the Scriptures that there are specific methods that evil will increase, which will prevail over the earth for a time; however, hasn't that been continuously the case? In the first century, the apostle John wrote that "the entire world depends on the power of the wicked one" (1 Jn. 5:19). It might depend on the power of the wicked one now. However, it does not come from him! It is a usurped rule that will be restored to its rightful owner-- the Lord, who paid the supreme rate with His own life to redeem it. As Psalm 24:1 declares, "The earth is the Lord's, and all it consists of, the world, and those who dwell in it." That is the truth that we need to identify to live by.

The main inroad that the opponent has into our lives, our households, our schools, and our world, is through worry. We must take a stand versus the worry that the opponent is looking for to increase over the whole world to enhance his control. We need to identify that we will not let fear dictate the course of our lives or our present actions. We are at war with fear.

As President Roosevelt said, "We have nothing to fear, however, fear itself." If we grow in faith, we can win this war. Real faith is not an uncertain confidence in ourselves; it results from a living relationship with the God who enjoys us, has called us, and will empower us to do all that He created us to do.

The Lord Jesus said that completion of the age is the harvest (see Mt. 13:39). The world is currently experiencing the excellent- est ingathering of souls into the Kingdom in history. Nevertheless, as we likewise comprehend, the harvest is likewise the time when everything that has been sown in man will come to complete maturity, both the excellent and the evil. This is why we see in such Scripture passages as Isaiah 60:1 -5 that the light and splendor are appearing upon the Lord's individuals at the very time when "darkness" and even "deep darkness" will cover the earth. At the end of this age, we can expect to see the ultimate yoke of chains of fear coming to its complete maturity, at the same time the Lord's people are experiencing the most significant levels of faith and peace.

We are about to experience the best fear and the most significant faith ever launched on the earth. These will be happening at the very same time. If we are not growing in faith also evidenced by growing in the peace of God, we will be growing in fear and the stress and anxiety that will eventually even trigger males' hearts to stop working. The ultimate response to combating fear is growing in faith, and God's peace that goes beyond understanding.

We must first brighten the evil nature of fear and how it is used to position a wide variety of shackles on our life. This illumination alone will start to break that fear off of our lives. The opponent dwells in darkness, and whenever the light exposes him, it rapidly starts unraveling his power. We desire to change every worry in our life with a biblical, step-by-step method for growing in the faith, love, and peace of God.

CHAPTER ELEVEN

Seeking Peace: The Recent Phase

Going Back To Middle East diplomacy in the post-1967 period, together with UN efforts, those of the Arab states, the PLO, the USSR, and the European allies were frequently rebuffed. These initiatives shared two vital features that were inappropriate to Washington. They made at least some gesture towards Palestinian national rights; 2nd, they called for meaningful international involvement in a settlement. The reason for the U.S. rejection of such proposals has already been sorted out. The Palestinians perform no services for the United States, certainly are an irritant because their predicament stirs up Arab nationalist sentiments; therefore, they lack rights. And the United States is reluctant to accept disturbance outdoors in a region successfully drawn under the Monroe Doctrine, much as Kissinger had explained.

By 1988 it was challenging for the U.S. federal government and the media to hide PLO and other Arab initiatives for a political settlement. By December, the U.S. federal government had become something of an international laughing-stock with its increasingly desperate efforts to reject the apparent.

Washington grudgingly accepted "declare victory," claiming that at last, the PLO had been obliged to utter George Shultz's "magic words." The function of the exercise, Shultz discussed to Reagan, was to make sure optimum humiliation. In his knowledge on apologia, Turmoil and Triumph, Shultz reports that he informed Reagan in December 1988 that Arafat was stating in one location "' Unc, unc, unc,' and in another he was stating, 'cle, cle, cle,' but he never bring himself to say 'Uncle,'" in style anticipated of the lesser breeds. Likewise, Shultz needed that the PLO not just condemn terrorism but "renounce" it, therefore yielding that it had taken part in terrorism. However, at a level hardly noticeable in comparison to the record put together by Shultz and his predecessors, another unmentionable truth. Once again, the function was to grind a helpless and weak adversary underfoot, which frequently gives terrific enjoyment to the effective and makes them much regard. PLO requires renouncing violence "on a shared basis" have constantly been dismissed out of hand, as ludicrous.

It is, by the way, beside inconceivable that U.S. news reporting or commentary may keep in mind of the major UN resolution on terrorism, which mentions "that nothing in the present resolution could in any method prejudice the right to self-determination, independence, and liberty, as stemmed from the Charter of the United Nations, of individuals forcibly deprived of that right, particularly peoples under colonial and racist regimes and foreign occupation or other forms of colonial domination, nor the right of these individuals to have a hard time to this end

186

and to receive and seek support [following the Charter and other principles of worldwide law]" The resolution passed 153-2, U.S. and Israel opposed, Honduras alone abstaining. It is therefore banned, and banned from history.

Naturally, Washington rejects any ideal to withstand the terror and injustice enforced by its customers. Since Washington's stand is undoubtedly legitimate by U.S. commentators, undoubtedly axiomatic, there is no requirement to report the truths, or what they suggest about the occupied territories or southern Lebanon, which is apparent enough. On these matters, silence has been overall, apart from margins of the usual margins, and the most elementary conclusions would by now be essentially unintelligible to a U.S. (undoubtedly, Western) audience.

It is only reasonable to keep in mind, in this connection, that Israeli practice is even more truthful. After four hundred Hamas activists were deported in December 1992, a leadership post in the Israeli press observed that "we can not accuse [Hamas] of practicing random horror which hits innocent females and kids, because they don't"; "we should attend to the fact that ... all Hamas guerrilla operations before the expulsion were targeted at soldiers." The same point was made about Hezbollah by Uzi Mahanaimi, a respected hawkish commentator on Intelligence and Arab Affairs. Talking about Israel's attack on Lebanon in July 1993, he asserted that "Hezbollah is not a terror organization," considering that it avoids striking civilians except in retaliation for Israeli attacks on Lebanese civilians. Moreover, 'Hezbollah separates in between the Israeli conquest of Southern Lebanon and the presence of the State of Israel," taking its task to be just that of reversing the conquest, that is, legitimate resistance against an army inhabiting foreign area in offense of Security Council orders. Other commentators mock the U.S. State Department, "which knows no better than to provide Hezbollah higher status by declaring it 'the most obvious horror company in the world.'" American commentary, in contrast, keeps strictly to State Department doctrine.

Mahanaimi's analysis, undoubtedly right, simultaneously raises the concern of why Israel has demanded occupying southern Lebanon. Not for security factors, as both the history and his precise observations make clear. A widespread suspicion is that his needs to do, when again, with long-term strategies for control over the region's water resources, much as in the case of the "little trick" about Labor Party settlement programs from the 970s exposed by Haim Gvirtzman. However, in the absence of any closer query, the questions stay open.

Returning to the shenanigans of December 1988, the record reveals clearly that the gap between the U.S. and PLO positions stayed about as before on every major issue. The farce continued smoothly in the public arena. Having stated victory, the United

States could then impose its analysis of what had taken place and proceed on course, without worry of contradiction.

As a benefit for saying "uncle" inappropriately modest tones, the PLO was offered the right to participate in a "dialogue" with the U.S. ambassador in Tunis. Publishing leaked procedures of the very first meeting; the Jerusalem Post could hardly contain its satisfaction over the fact that "the American representative adopted the Israeli positions." Ambassador Robert Pelletreau stated two crucial conditions that the PLO should accept: it must abandon the idea of a worldwide conference, and call off the "riots" in the occupied territories (the Intifada), "which we view as terrorist acts versus Israel." Simply put, the PLO must guarantee that the previous status quo is restored, so that Israel's repression and expansion in the territories with firm U.S. assistance could once again continue unhindered. The ban on an international conference follows that the world is out of action. Participation of outside celebrations beyond the United States and its clients would lead to undesirable pressure for a non rejectionist political settlement. Britain might be permitted later on, Russia, however, no voice that might prove too independent. The characterization of the Intifada as "terrorism" (for example, tax resistance in Beit Sahour, efficiently stated invalid by the United States at the Security Council a year later follows from the U.S.-Israeli rejection of the otherwise consentaneous worldwide consensus on the right of resistance to military occupation, already gone over. The "large accumulation of unlimited humiliations and casually committed cruelties" that close Israeli observers consider the "important factor" generating resistance has been removed from the record together with the global agreement on "fear.".

A couple of weeks later, in February 1989, Rabin had a conference with 5 Peace Now leaders in which he expressed his satisfaction with the U.S.-PLO discussion. He described it as an "effective operation," reporter Nahum Barnea reported, including just "low-level conversations" that avoid any serious issue. The Americans are "now satisfied, and do not look for any [political] option, and they will give us a year, at least a year," to deal with the scenario in our method. By doing this is force. "The inhabitants of the territories go through severe military and economic pressure," Rabin discussed. "In the end, they will be broken," and will accept Israel's terms.

Backing the essentials of this view, a top-level U.S. official urged Israel to put an end to its public objections to the dialogue, which "just add significance" to it, hence hindering its designated objective: to displace attention from the strong repression of the Intifada. In early March, Bush administration proposals, using "ideas" to Israel and the PLO, highlighted the point. Israel was advised to restrict the repressive procedures set up to suppress the Intifada, and the PLO to end the "violent demonstrations" and the circulation of "inflammatory leaflets."

The proposal, then, is that the PLO cooperate with Israel in developing a somewhat harsher, but not too severe differences of the former status quo.

The methods embraced in December 1988 worked like a charm. News protection of the occupied areas declined further, thus granting Israel the chance to turn to still harsher steps so that "they will be broken" as ultimately, they were; there is a limitation to what flesh and blood can endure, when any hope of assistance from the outside is gone. Attention was concentrated on the U.S.-managed "peace process," not the repression heightening with U.S. backing. Nonviolent resistance was lastly displaced by violence, much to the relief of U.S. and Israeli authorities, who have constantly been particularly concerned about the risk of small amounts, as Israeli analysts have long acknowledged.

The violence of the Israeli response to the Intifada got some general notice; however, neither these reports, nor the periodic accounts in earlier years when atrocities passed beyond the norm, offer a precise photo of the "large accumulation of limitless humiliations and delicately committed cruelties" that lastly led to the uprising. More illuminating are the innumerable cases thought about too insignificant to report, for example, an occasion in Gaza a couple of weeks before the Intifada broke out there. A Palestinian girl, Intissar al-Atar, was shot and killed in a schoolyard by a resident of a neighboring Jewish settlement.

The murderer, Shimon Yifrah, was apprehended a month later on and launched on bail because the courts determined that "the offense is not severe adequate" to require detention. In September 1989, he was acquitted of all charges other than triggering death by carelessness. The judge concluded that he only meant to shock the girl by firing his weapon at her in a schoolyard, not to kill her, so "this is not a case of a criminal individual who needs to be punished, deterred, and taught a lesson by imprisoning him." Yifrah was given a seven-month suspended sentence, while inhabitants in the courtroom broke out in tune and dance.

Below the limit of attention in the United States, these events left some memories amongst Israelis. As inhabitant violence against Arabs installed in the months after the Oslo Agreement together with the "need that the Israeli-Jewish public, and especially the government, ought to understand the spiritual inhabitants in these tough times they are going through," OlekNetzer recommended another appearance at a photo of the settlers "who danced in a circle of happiness with Uzi [rifles] on their shoulders" after Yifrah's release, and who now "fear that they will no longer be able to kill individuals, especially children, and be immune from penalty." Such cases and their reaction in the United States provide a bargain more understanding than the periodic massacre that is too violent to ignore. They also supply insight into the values that inspire U.S. leaders to decline the right of resistance and declare it to be terrorism against U.S. clients, standing alone versus the world.

While Rabin's "extreme military and financial pressure" had the intended impacts on the subject population, Washington monitored a version of the "peace procedure" that would satisfy the two basic requirements: no meaningful outside interference, and no Palestinian rights. On May 14, 1989, Israel's coalition Labor-Likud (Peres-Shamir) government adopted an in-depth "peace plan," with three basic concepts:

1) There can be no "additional Palestinian state in the Gaza district and the area between Israel and Jordan" (Jordan currently being a "Palestinian state");

2)" There will be no change in the status of Judea, Samaria and Gaza other than following the standard guidelines of the [Israeli] Government," which rejects an "extra Palestinian state."

3)" Israel will not conduct settlements with the PLO," though it might concur to speak to certain Palestinians other than their picked political agents.

On these conditions, "complimentary elections" were held under Israeli military control, with much of the Palestinian leadership in jail without charge or expelled.

The United States backed the Israeli proposal while keeping its essential content under wraps. There appears to have been no main reference to the May 14 plan, nor any report in journalism. However, it was the operative policy statement, and this was comprehended in Washington, where the May initiative was lauded for its "terrific guarantee and potential." 70 Secretary of State James Baker revealed in October that "our goal the whole time has been to attempt to help in applying the Shamir effort. There is no other proposition or effort that we are working with." A different "Shamir initiative" had been proposed in April, then superseded by the May 14 Shamir-Peres Election Plan, which was the only "proposal or effort" that Israel had presented formally, and was for that reason, the only "Shamir effort" that Baker or anyone else was working with.

In December 1989, the Department of State released the five-point Baker Plan, which stated that Israel would attend a "dialogue" in Cairo with Egypt and Palestinians acceptable to the United States and Israel. These Palestinians would be permitted to talk about execution of the Israeli propositions, however nothing else: "The Palestinians will come to the discussion prepared to go over elections and the negotiating procedure following Israel's effort and would be free to raise issues that associated to their viewpoints on how to make elections and the negotiating procedure succeed."

In brief, the Palestinian delegation would be permitted to express viewpoints on the technical features of Israel's proposition to disallow any significant type of Palestinian self-determination, and even this right was accorded just to Palestinians who encourage Israel and its patron that they are complimentary from any taint of association with the PLO. The purpose of the latter condition was again a little bit more than humiliation. It has been comprehended on all sides that these associations exist, in which the PLO was directing the negotiating process.

The Bush-Baker plan, then, was to have the Intifada squashed by force while attention was diverted to a "peace procedure" that bars Palestinian rights. While pursuing this two-part program to deal with the Israel-Palestinian issue, the Bush-Baker team pushed forward with their policies in the Gulf, extending still even more their support for Saddam Hussein, relatively unconcerned to his appalling record of atrocities. In Octobe 1989, as the Baker Plan was being offered its final type, the White House intervened in an extremely secret meeting to ensure that Iraq would get another $1 billion in loan warranties eliminating Treasury and Commerce department objections that Iraq was not creditworthy. The reason the State Departmen discussed, was that Iraq was "essential to U.S. interests in the Middle East"; it was "influential in the peace process" and was "a secret to maintaining stability in the area, using terrific trade opportunities for US business." A few weeks later on, as U.S invasion forces were bombarding slums in Panama, the White House revealed plans to lift a ban on loans to Saddam, executed quickly after-- to attain the "objective of increasing U.S. exports and put us in a better position to handle Iraq regarding its human rights record, the State Department explained with a straight face.

Once once again, to comprehend the performance of American democracy, it is worth noting that practically absolutely nothing that has simply been examined worrying the Bush-Baker programs reached the general public, apart from the dissident margins, where a record of the ongoing events was readily available to a tiny portion of the population.

Bush administration aid to Saddam Hussein continued until the day of his intrusion of Kuwait in August 1990. At that point, policy moved in the way currently discussed, as the administration seized the opportunity to establish much more firmly U.S. control of the oil-producing areas by a force program.

The war's consequences offered both a chance and a need to rejuvenate the "peace process." The requirement arose from the Gulf's sordid spectacle: huge damage and casualties, the human rights disaster intensifying under the effect of sanctions; the Gulf tyrannies secured from democratic pressures; Saddam Hussein securely in power, having demolished popular rebellions with indirect U.S. support. All in all, hardly a scene that might be left in public memory, especially after the craze of jingoist hysteria and wonder for the Grand Leader that had been worked up by the doctrinal organizations.

The chance emerged from the international context. At last, Europe had completely conceded the Middle East to the United States; Europeans would henceforth avoid independent initiatives, restricting themselves to implementation of U.S. rejectionist teaching, as Norway certainly did in 1993. The Soviet Union was gone, its remnants now faithful customers of Washington. The UN had ended up being virtually a U.S. company. Whatever space the superpower dispute used for independent nonalignment was gone, and the catastrophe of commercialism that swept the standard colonial domains of the West in the 1980s left the Third World mired in general misery, disciplined by forces of the Western-managed "market." With Arab nationalism dealt yet another squashing blow by Saddam's aggression and terror and PLO techniques of more than the normal ineptitude, the Arab rulers had less require than before to react to popular pressures with pro-Palestinian gestures. The United States was, for that reason, in an excellent position to advance its rejectionist program without interference, moving towards the option laid out by James Baker well before the Gulf crisis while satisfying the fundamental conditions stressed by Henry Kissinger years previously, now change by changed conditions. Europe, having deserted any independent function, was less of a threat. Russia could now be welcomed rather than history's "Greatest Prize" excluded, loyal, and powerless. The PLO approached the same status, for similar reasons, by mid-1993.

The "peace process" was restored with terrific excitement at Madrid in the fall of 1991. The "exceptional tableau" in Madrid exposed "that a very good deal had changed," Times diplomatic correspondent R. W. Apple observed, as "George Bush and the United States today plucked the fruits of victory in the Persian Gulf war." The reason Bush might now "dream such great dreams" about Middle East peace, Apple discussed, is that his "vision of the future" can be implemented without any fear that "regional tensions" may cause superpower confrontation, and "no longer should the United States contend with countries whose cantankerousness was reinforced by Moscow's interest in continuing discontent"-- the basic referral to Soviet adherence to the worldwide consensus that the United States declines, in magnificent isolation.

U.S. diplomats naturally agreed. As the Madrid negotiations opened, Alfred Leroy Atherton, in charge of Near East affairs in the State Department under Ford and Carter and a participant in the Camp David settlements, observed that "no significant Arab-Israeli arrangement, a minimum of since 1967, has actually been reached without an active U.S. function, and this need still exists." Now, he continued, "the U.S. task will certainly be much easier in the absence of a Soviet spoiling role." That an active U.S. function has been essential is correct. Simply as in the Caribbean affairs, absolutely nothing else is allowed by the ruling superpower; that, after all, is the standard significance of the Monroe Doctrine, understood for Latin America in 1945 and reached the Middle East. It is also true that the previous Soviet Union had played a "spoiling function," signing up with the rest of the world (consisting of Europe) in challenging U.S. rejectionist styles.

Experts found "fantastic inspiration" in Bush's statement that "the time has come to put an end to the Arab-Israeli dispute," words "talked with commitment by an American president at the height of his powers" and forming part of his "broad vision of Middle East peace-building" (Helena Cobban). Even critics were impressed. Anthony Lewis composed that the president is "at the height of his powers" and "has made very clear that he wishes to breathe light into that theoretical creature, the Middle East peace process." The reasons that the animal remained theoretical are unarticulated, unthinkable. Palestinian Middle East scholar WalidKijalidi, an adviser to the Jordanian-Palestinian delegation, hailed "the personal dedication of the U.S. president to a simple and extensive settlement." In the occupied territories, educated Palestinians reported, there were fantastic expectations and hope.

Something else that "had altered," the press exulted, was "the birth of a brand-new pragmatism among the Palestinians," now raised "another important notch" through Baker's benign influence at Madrid (Thomas Friedman). Until Madrid, Friedman continued, "both sides have hidden behind the argument that there is nobody on the other side with whom to work out" the official variation of the fact that the PLO called on Israel to negotiate; however, the United States and Israel refused. The Palestinian delegation at Madrid called "clearly for a two-state service," Friedman wrote admiringly, so different from the abhorred PLO, which supported (or maybe "prepared") the Security Council resolution calling for a two-state solution fifteen years earlier. Madrid's excellent accomplishment was "the Palestinian self-adjustment to the real-life," Palestinian acceptance of "a duration of autonomy under continued Israeli supremacy," throughout which Israel can build the realities of its irreversible dominance with U.S. help, as it proceeded to do after Madrid. This determination to follow U.S. orders-- the real world-- has "tossed the negative stereotypes out the window," Times reporter Clyde Haberman observed approvingly. With their "brand-new pragmatism."

Palestinians are at last prepared "to talk with Israel, to set aside all-or-nothing needs, to accept half a loaf in the kind of interim self-rule under Israeli dominance." The Madrid conference was organized under unilateral U.S. management, an obsequious

Russian partner providing a fig-leaf of internationalism. The Palestinian delegation, after passing U.S.-Israeli tests of legitimacy, was informed by James Baker that the negotiations would be based exclusively on UN 242, which uses absolutely nothing to the Palestinians: "Anything else, the president kept in mind, would fail the twin tests of fairness and security." The adjustments in the global agreement through the 1970s, as reflected in the vetoed Security Council resolutions and other obstructed initiatives, were completely off the program. However, Baker did unwind the need in his December 1989 five point plan that Palestinians should strictly keep the technical information of Israel's program for integration of the territories.

As was fairly clear from the outset, the objective of the most current stage of the "peace process" has been to develop a peace settlement among the states of the region, with Palestinian national rights left out. The best result from Washington's perspective would be a settlement that entrenches the conventional strategic conception and offers it a public type raising implied understandings to an official treaty. Well and good if some version of regional autonomy can remove the Palestinian concern. Meanwhile, security arrangements amongst Israel, Turkey, Egypt, and the United States can be extended, perhaps bringing others in to accept the customer role. There need be no more concern over independent European or Third

World efforts, or Soviet support for attempts within the region to hinder such styles.

While the settlements were continuing without problem, Israel stepped up the harsh repression in the areas, following the believing detailed by then-Defense Minister Yitzhak Rabin in February 1989. These U.S.-Israeli measures achieved much success, extended with Rabin's "closure" of the areas, which administered a crushing blow to the staggering Palestinian economy and also took an essential step towards the meant "canonization" by effectively barring West Bank Palestinians from their organizations (health centers, etc.) in East Jerusalem, and avoiding travel from the northern to the southern part of the West Bank, considering that the main roadway connections pass through East Jerusalem.

The current circumstance is evaluated plausibly, in my opinion, by General (res.) Shlomo Gazit, previously head of Israeli military intelligence, a senior authorities of the military administration of the occupied territories, and a leading individual in the secret meetings that developed the Oslo Agreement's security arrangements. With the collapse of the Soviet Union, he composed, Israel's primary job has not altered at all, and it stays of essential value. Its area at the center of the Arab Muslim Middle East Moira is Israel to be a dedicated guardian of stability in all the nations surrounding it. It's [role] is to safeguard the existing routines: to prevent or stop the processes of radicalization and block the expansion of fundamentalist spiritual zealotry or any other form of "radical nationalism" that comes along. In this job, it is to be joined by U.S. allies, maybe more freely than in the past. These are generally the conclusions that had been articulated by American coordinators thirty-five years earlier. What has changed is that they no longer have to contend with a possible "ruining function" of outsiders who may assist in indigenous efforts to cause modifications undesirable to the rulers.

Subsequent shifts in U.S. policy add trustworthiness to Gazit's assessment.

Israeli analysts rapidly recognized the Clinton administration to be much more severe in the rejection of Palestinian rights than Israel's government. Political reporter AmnonBarzilai observed that the new Clinton administration's proposals to Israel and the Palestinians broke brand-new ground in rejectionism. For the very first time, they specified that "all the alternatives will be left open," consisting of even "the demand for full addition of the territories" under "Israeli sovereignty." In this regard, he notes, Clinton went well beyond the governing Labor Party, "which never demanded that all the choices be kept open," only "territorial compromise." The U.S. effort will, for that reason "strengthen the suspicion amongst the Palestinians that there is a factor to fear an Israeli conspiracy with American assistance," he writes; though in truth, neither the United States nor the

Israeli political blocs would consider the addition of the territories, for reasons already pointed out.

Reporting from Washington, Ron Ben-Yishai established the point further. He described the Clinton administration's new Middle East policy as "innovative," "a various diplomatic position from those of preceding Administrations," and one that is "entirely positive" from Israel's perspective. Senior U.S. government officials have made it clear that Arabs "will not be able to get concessions from Israel through American pressure, diplomatic or financial." Similarly, Ben-Yishai continued, security relations were boosted, consisting of arrangements kept secret. "Never have we had such great relations with an American administration," a senior Israeli authorities observed. According to Washington, thinking, the disappearance of the Soviet Union, removing any alternative choices for the Arab states, is one of numerous factors leading American policy in this instructions. Clinton experts "see the [increased] support for Israel as part of a much broader international conception that includes a brand-new view of the Middle East in the era after the Cold War and the Gulf war," now that U.S. dominance of the region is more firmly established than before. The new technique to "Israel and its next-door neighbors," "the western part of the region," is matched by the new technique to "the eastern part": the policy of "dual containment" intended at both Iraq and Iran, formerly played one versus the other. "It is necessary to stress that there is no political leader in Israel, and likewise not in Riyadh or Kuwait, who would take any exception to this global conception."

The same may be true of Cairo and other capitals, which have reasons to pin the blame on malign outsiders (Iran, Sudan, and others) for violence and disturbance that lead to large measures from their own social and financial policies.

Ben-Yishai pointed out the significance of Clinton's appointments for the Middle East, notably his choice as chief Middle East adviser and "one of the peace team's main figures, Martin Indyk, up until [January 1993] the head of the Washington Institute for Near East Policy." Before Clinton's inauguration, "Indyk and the deputy director of the Institute, Robert Satloff, had presented to Clinton's transition group a policy memorandum on a brand-new Middle East policy," now being implemented under Indyk's instructions. Indyk, an Australian who was approved citizenship a couple of days before his visit, was a worker of the Israeli lobby (AIPAC), mainly representing the policy spectrum's hawkish right-wing. Indyk left AIPAC to found the Institute to counter the impact of Washington think tanks that the lobby considered pro-Arab and anti-Israel. Some even have recommended that the United States consider joining the international agreement on a peaceful diplomatic settlement. The Institute has played an nteresting function in American cultural life. It makes it possible for press reporters to present U.S.-Israeli propaganda while maintaining their fabled neutrality, "merely reporting the realities" while citing some "professional" offered by the institute to provide the opinions they want propagate.

Clinton policies conformed to the picture presented by Israeli experts. Among the administration's very first jobs was to deal with the embarrassment brought on by Israel's deportation of four hundred Palestinians in December 1992. The deportees were accused of responsibility for "terrorist acts," particularly attacks versus the inhabiting Israeli army that can not be called terrorist," as acknowledged in the Israeli press. Danny Rubinstein observed that about half the declared "Hamas activists" operated in Islamic spiritual organizations, including preachers, instructors, "a huge number of youths who function as missionaries for increasing religious practice," and specialists who "assisted establish the Islamic motion's network of academic and well-being organizations that includes clinics, kindergartens, kitchens for the clingy, and companies providing aid to detainees' households, orphans, and invalids." "Members of the military wing of Hamas and the Islamic Jihad organization are not among those deported," he included. The analysis was verified in a study by Middle East Watch, which found that half the deportees were imams, spiritual scholars, or hari'a (Islamic law) judges, consisting of the head of the

Palestine Religious Scholars Association, an imam at Al-Aqsa Mosque. In contrast, others are university teachers, medica professionals (sixteen on the UNRWA personnel), schoo teachers, entrepreneurs, students, and manual employees Courts had actually convicted four, and eight others had been in administrative detention (imprisoning without charge or trial) A "significant percentage of the deportees had never been convicted of offenses," something of an understatement. Middle East Watch described conditions in the "snake-pit" where they had been transferred in Lebanon as harmful and disgraceful and when again hired Israel to end this "serious breach of the Fourth Geneva Convention." Israeli intelligence concurred with these evaluations. Ha'aretz priced estimate a "senio government official" who stated that the intelligence service (Shabak) provided Prime Minister Yitzhak Rabin with six name of Hamas activists, including one more when they were asked "to increase the number." Israeli intelligence was "astonished to discover that more than four hundred had been expelled-with no appropriate intelligence info.

The American press had no usage for any of this, choosing th New York Times' variation by Israeli Arabist Ehud Yaari, a partner of Indyk's Washington Institute. According to Yaari who ignores the intelligence reports and other Israeli sources "About 300 of the 413 deportees made up Hamas's comman network in the West Bank and Gaza Strip." His account make some sense on the assumptions expressed by Cabinet Legal Advisor Yosef Harish, arguing for the expulsion before Israel's High Court: asked the number of homeowners of the occupied areas are members of terrorist organizations, he responded, "I think all of them."

The Security Council passed a resolution demanding that the deportees be returned forthwith. Israel declined, stating that it would permit them to return as it chose. The Clinton administration then determined that Israel was honoring the Security Council resolution by flagrantly breaching it. The problem was stated closed, and without delay, disappeared from press protection, which returned to the "peace procedure." The Washington Institute's much-quoted professional Robert Satloff discussed that Palestinians need to be heartened by the administration's decision to back Israel's defiance of the UN: "It's to the Palestinians' negotiating benefit that the U.S. and the Israelis have the relationship they have now."

While not as revolutionary as Ben-Yishai indicates, the policy modifications are instructional and fascinating nonetheless. The conventional tactical conceptions and objectives are not being abandoned with the Soviet Union; rather, as General Gazit observed, they are being pursued more vigorously, the deterrent having disappeared and the Third World becoming much more unprotected for this and other reasons. The pattern is exactly what we have seen somewhere else in the world. It is significantly irregular with years of propaganda about the Cold War, but quite in accord with both preparation and history with the basic thinking that has supported the policy. The method events have unfolded.

Conclusion

Even skeptics and debunkers need to admit that often no matter how "crazy" the so-called "conspiracy theories" sound, there are undeniable facts at their structure. It's a full-time task to separate the fiction's realities when discussing conspiracy theories or the Illuminati given that there is so much disinformation, false information, half-truths, and hoaxes out there. I hope this book has helped you in your Pursuit understand the fact and revealed strong, verifiable details that have helped you increase your knowledge.

For over the years, I've been tirelessly investigating this topic and thoroughly putting together the puzzle pieces to develop an accurate picture of this huge secret.

Elitism has continuously been the dark side of illuminism; the innovative vanguard that seizes control since it knows what's great for individuals, the philosopher-king who knows the reality, the technocrat who knows how to run wars and societies, all try to hoard the light at the top of the pyramid. Factor, which can be used to rescue man from churches and kings, can likewise be used to enslave him with dogmas of its own. Knowledge is power that can be abused."

Elitists and Big Government New World Order promoters desire individuals to believe that rights originated from the government instead of God. The United States Declaration of Independence says, "Our Creator endows all men with particular unalienable rights," which suggests our rights can't be eliminated and are irreversible from the moment we are born. No society can vote to stop them; no government can offer you cash in exchange for approving them; they are fundamental, irreversible, and unchangeable. The State (the government) is God in the New World Order, so most bureaucrats and the mainstream media portray presidents as contemporary day. The Illuminati desire the government to be the supreme authority, not God. They desire your loyalty to be to them, not to your family, community, or spiritual belief. The law is thought about the Gospel. The government is your protector, instructor, and service provider.

Because of the 24-hour cable news and satellite networks, the Internet, and social media, numerous individuals are inclined to think that we can Quickly resolve all the world's issues because we are instantly informed about them; however, this info age appears to be a double-edged sword. On one level, this innovation notifies us about significant events or issues, but at the same time, it usually prevents people from acting to solve them. The term narcotizing dysfunction describes the theory that because modern-day media, when people are notified about a particular problem, they replace working to fix it, for just understanding it.

Cultural Marxism creates an unnoticeable pressure that prevents many people from breaking away from the crowd and keeps almost everybody following the herd and subscribing to society's norms and is scared to question the deeply ingrained patterns of their peers.

Many individuals who criticize "conspiracy theorists" claim that all of us have a "confirmation bias," which is the tendency for individuals to prefer info that supports their existing worldview or hypothesis, which in most cases is an accurate evaluation of conspiracy theorists. However, this isn't the case for me. For numerous years after the 9/11 attacks on the World Trade Center, I believed the official account of what occurred. I thought the conspiracy theory about Iraq having weapons of mass damage was prepared to use against us anytime.

We know that searching for the fact is unpleasant and challenging, not to discuss time-consuming; most people never even begin on the journey. Instead they turn their mind, body, and soul over to the mesmerizing traditional media or celebrity news or sports home entertainment, so I praise you on your decision to be different and for taking the roadway less taken a trip. I hope I've been able to supply you a few of the responses you've been seeking since I too have a burning desire to know the fact, and we are on the same course.

In this book, we've covered a variety of evidence, ranging from the Illuminati's original works, to how they were discovered, what their strategies are, and tracking them to their Skull & Bones, Bohemian Grove, and the Bilderberg Group offspring.

212

We've seen some obscure expert discoveries, checked out their approaches, signs, and more, which, when thoroughly assembled, an indisputable image proving the Illuminati is stil alive.

CPSIA information can be obtained
at www.ICGtesting.com
Printed in the USA
BVHW040813060421
604317BV00002B/166

9 781801 114400